When You
WALK
Through a
STORM

Jeris Bragan

Pacific Press Publishing Association
Boise, Idaho
Oshawa, Ontario, Canada

Edited by Marvin Moore
Designed by Tim Larson
Cover photo by David Rogers
Typeset in 10/12 Century Schoolbook

Unless otherwise noted, all Scripture quotations in this book
are from the Holy Bible: New International Version.

Library of Congress Cataloging-in-Publication Data

Bragan, Jeris, E., 1946–
When you walk through a storm: a prisoner makes sense
out of suffering /Jeris Bragan.
127 p. cm.
1. Suffering—Religious aspects—Christianity. 2. Prisoners
—Religious life. 3. Bragan, Jeris E., 1946– . I. Title.
BT732.7.B69 199190-62279
CIP
248.8'6'092—dc20

ISBN 0-8163-0936-1

91 92 93 94 95 • 5 4 3 2

Contents

Introduction

In August 1988, I began conducting a fiction writing workshop at the Tennessee State Prison in Nashville. I did this on a volunteer basis, primarily out of a sense that my life was passing from one phase to another, and this was a good way to mark that passage. I had just sold what would become my first published novel. I was finally seeing my aspirations of writing full time fulfilled, and I wanted to share my love of writing, of the work of putting words on paper, with people who would appreciate it. It seemed to me that incarcerated men might value someone working with them more than those who usually inhabit "creative writing" classes. This was a way, I felt, of giving something back.

That was two years ago. The workshop has shrunk from a beginning group of twenty men down to less than five. Of the original members of the group, only two remain. One of them is Jeris Bragan.

My first impressions of Jeris on that hot day in August, when I anxiously let myself be processed from one checkpoint to another, stick in my mind very clearly. From the beginning, it seemed, there was something about him that didn't quite fit. The other students were pros. Most of these guys had been in prison before. Several were lifelong criminals and made no bones about it.

But there was, and continues to be, something about Jeris Bragan that just doesn't fit the mold. He doesn't fit in with the rest of the population. That's made his life in prison harder at times.

Jeris Bragan is physically imposing, a large man with a ruddy Irish face, blond hair, and a voice that's low and deep, yet surprisingly soft for a man his size. He wears the con's uniform: blue work shirt and denim pants with a white stripe down each leg. He's in his fourteenth year of incarceration.

Yet somehow, prison isn't etched in his face like so many of the others. Contrary to popular belief, crime is not an easy way to make a living. Many men in prison look older than their years. They've lived hard lives, and they show every second of their time on this earth.

Prison life is hard as well, but as an inmate explained to me once, the strain of prison isn't so much the confinement, but the overwhelming tedium of routine. It's not so much that prison is some kind of awful hellhole that reduces a man to rubble overnight, but rather that prison is so all-fired *gray,* so mind-numbingly monotonous. Each day passes like the one before it, and tomorrow will be just like today.

Most prisoners walk around without much expression. In prison, it doesn't serve one well to let on too much. To a "free-world" person (a term the cons use for those who can walk out at the end of the day) the place seems strangely diffident, and suspiciously calm. From a distance, the 100-year-old Tennessee State Penitentiary looks like Disneyland. But if there's any fantasy at all in there, it's more in the nature of a nightmare.

The last thing I ever expected that first day was to walk into a classroom at the prison school building and have one of the inmates hand me an already-published book. The book was *Detective in Search of Grace.* I'd never heard of the book, and I'd never heard of Jeris Bragan.

"Grace strikes during times of great pain and restlessness," he inscribed on the flyleaf. "It also strikes during times of great peace and joy. May yours be the latter kind. Either way, it's a blessing."

"From your friend behind the walls," he signed it. "Shalom!"

I remember being struck by the show of warmth and intimacy from someone I'd only just met. It wasn't at all what I'd expected, but then many things about Jeris have surprised me.

Ever since Jeris became a writer behind walls, he's always been prolific. By the time I met him, he'd already written and published two books. He's published articles in the inspirational press at such a rate that one magazine had to ask him to hold off for a while; he was showing up in every issue.

People from all over the world correspond with him. Many seek his advice and guidance with questions of religion and spirituality and faith. Many people have been inspired by him, and through his example have found their own faith renewed and strengthened.

Pretty good track record for a convicted murderer!

The con who proclaims his innocence or finds Jesus in jail, or both, is almost a cliche. Religious conversions that occur as one's parole hearing nears are surprisingly convenient. When Jeris mentioned almost casually one day that he was innocent of the murder of which he was convicted, all my alarms went off. A lifelong cynic and, until recently, a confirmed agnostic, I thought, "Yeah, here it comes."

Only it didn't. The "con" job that I expected never came. And I couldn't help but notice that even as he related how he came to be an innocent man in prison for life, there was a surprising lack of anger.

In fact, as I came to know Jeris better, the realization grew stronger that here was a man at peace with himself and with God. Stripped of everything—reputation, worldly goods, physical freedom, citizenship, almost everything we hold dear—this guy was, amazingly enough, *happy!*

How could this be?

Jeris Bragan's story reads like bad fiction. There has been in his life such a convoluted, bizarre, random set of circumstances, coincidences, and contrived ironies that if a movie were to be made of the events that led him to his present situation, no one would believe it. A story like his can't be made up; it has to come from real life.

The facts in Jeris Bragan's case are complex; some are

clear, some have become clouded over time. A few facts related to the case may never be known, but this much is: In 1976, Jeris Bragan lived in Chattanooga, Tennessee. He was a private detective and owned his own agency, a company called Searchers Corp. On Monday, November 22, 1976, Jeris's partner in the agency, an ex-CIA agent named George Urice, suffered a violent death in the agency's office. In April 1977 Jeris and his then-wife, Darleen, were arrested for murder. The following September, Jeris was convicted of first-degree murder and immediately sentenced to ninety-nine years. Darleen received a fifteen-to-twenty year sentence for second-degree murder.

The more I heard about the case, the more interested I became. And as I dug more, researched more, and read more, the portrait that emerged was of a man innocent of murder.

Jeris maintains that he wasn't even in his office the evening of George Urice's death. He says that Darleen came to their apartment, which was only a few doors down from the office, in a panic. George had fallen down, she said. He was drunk. She thought he was dead.

When Jeris got to the office, he found that George's hands had been handcuffed behind him. Darleen said she was alone with Urice in the office, and he was drunk. They had an argument, he attacked her, and she pushed him. Urice fell over backward, striking his head against a chair. She was afraid of him and put the handcuffs on him to protect herself. She was taking him over to their apartment when he stumbled and fell down a flight of stairs to his death.

In any case, when Jeris arrived on the scene he covered for his wife. They removed the handcuffs and dumped them in Lake Chickamauga, along with a fiberglass nightstick that had been lying nearby. Then they went back to the office and tried to set the scene to make it look like an accident.

This was, for Jeris, an error in judgment that he pays for even today. He lied to the police, destroyed evidence, obstructed justice, and later perjured himself on the stand. To this, he pleads guilty. But he maintains—and there is much to back him up on this—that he did not kill George Urice.

For what it's worth, I believe him.

The Hamilton County jury that heard Jeris's perjured testimony almost believed him as well. For one thing, the district attorney's office never did establish in court how Jeris was supposed to have murdered Urice. They first claimed that he had beaten Urice to death with brass knuckles, but the medical examiner testified that this was inconsistent with Urice's injuries. Then they claimed Jeris had killed Urice with a nightstick, but the medical examiner refuted that argument for the same reason. No actual method was ever established by which Jeris was supposed to have killed Urice.

On what basis, then, was Jeris convicted? A jailhouse snitch testified that Jeris admitted to him that he killed George Urice. The witness, a career criminal by the name of William Harold Torbett, known to his friends as "Buggy," also testified that he had not made a deal with the prosecutors in exchange for his testimony. But a short time later, the charges against Buggy, which could have resulted in a life sentence under the state's career criminal statutes, were dropped. He pleaded guilty to lesser charges and was sentenced to a term in the local workhouse. Then he escaped. The warrant for that escape was either pulled or lost, and for twelve years nobody was looking for Torbett, until a recent series of investigative articles in the *Chattanooga Times* brought this to light. Suddenly the local district attorney, still in office fourteen years later, decided to issue a warrant charging Torbett with escape!

Bragan claims to have never seen Buggy Torbett till the day they met in court. In recent years Nashville attorney Fred Steltemeier has investigated Jeris's case at his own expense. In 1988 he tracked Torbett to an Atlanta suburb, where he interviewed him. Torbett told Steltemeier that the DA's office *did* cut a deal with him in exchange for his testimony at the trial, and that he lied on the witness stand about his association with Jeris, but he said he was afraid to come back to Tennessee. Somebody, he said, would make sure he never testified.

Jeris Bragan's legal troubles were a severe test of his faith. His frustration levels have risen noticeably since he remarried in April 1989. But it seems he could always find a sign that his predicament had not gone unnoticed. The reaffirmation of his faith is a story best told by Jeris himself, in his many articles, his two other books, and in this volume. What began as a story of mistakes made, of despair and tragedy and stupidity and injustice, has become a story of one man's deepening awareness of the spiritual possibilities that exist within all of us. His has become a story of grace, of grace encountered and accepted under the worst possible circumstances imaginable.

"Someday they'll make a movie out of all this," he jokes, in a typical display of humor, "and they'll call it *Job II.*"

"One of the ways in which I've survived in this place," he told me, "is that I've never considered myself an inmate. Sure, I'm locked up. I can't go anywhere. But I refuse to accept that as a way of thinking. I'm imprisoned, and I've never been more free."

If you can find grace in the Tennessee State Penitentiary, then you can find it anywhere. During the two years that I've known Jeris, I've found some of my own hard-nosed cynicism melting. But as I've learned more about this case and watched Jeris in his struggle to win vindication these past two years, I've found myself tempted to despair at times that justice can ever win out. The system that convicted Jeris Bragan is not without sin itself, and those who run it are not above doing whatever they have to do in order to protect themselves.

In 1987, Jeris applied for executive clemency to the Tennessee Board of Paroles, which must pass on all such applications before they go to the governor's desk. Dozens of letters of support had been written to the board on Jeris's behalf, including even one from Tennessee State Prison Warden Mike Dutton himself.

Yet in spite of a spotless record and the many letters of support, Bragan's petition was denied. One of the men on the Board of Paroles later went on to a job with the district attorney's office in Chattanooga. Another man had been an associate warden at the women's prison before joining the Board of Paroles. In my file is an affidavit from a senior administrator at the women's prison, in which the administrator acknowledges that it was common knowledge around the facility that the associate warden in question was involved in a sexual affair with Bragan's wife while she served her time there. That man has now moved on to another job in the state Department of Corrections.

In late 1989, Jeris filed a petition for a Writ of Habeas Corpus with the federal court in Nashville, charging that his constitutional rights had been violated, and asking to have his case reviewed. In reviewing Bragan's claims, the courts found enough evidence of prosecutorial misconduct to appoint him an attorney and to hear arguments on both sides as to whether he should be granted a new trial. At the time of this writing, that case is still winding its way through the courts.

In the meantime, most Monday afternoons will find Jeris Bragan sitting in a classroom with a handful of working, struggling writers, myself included. He brings to the group an editorial eye as sharp as a surgeon's scalpel, a feel for structure, a sense of humor, and an overwhelming desire to make the most of a rotten situation. And one other thing.

Patience.

Steven Womack
September 3, 1990
Nashville, Tennessee

Prologue: In the Flames

W ould you like to dance?" Mary Ann asked me.

"I don't dance," I replied, sounding more abrupt than I intended. She looked hurt and I felt miserable. I kicked myself for asking her to the prom in the first place. Also, I wanted to kick Billy, my friend, for pressuring me to invite her.

"Nobody else will if you don't," he had insisted. "Besides, the prom will be on a Wednesday night, and you can go."

Mary Ann was bright and beautiful. Even though I felt awkward and uncertain about what to say around her, I liked her a lot. Everybody else did too. But it had seemed almost ghoulish to invite her to the senior prom of 1964! We all knew she was dying of leukemia. Although the disease was in temporary remission, her death was inevitable.

"It's OK," she said, squeezing my hand. "I forgot your church doesn't approve. We don't have to dance; I'm just happy to be here."

I breathed a sigh of relief, but her words slammed deep into my guts like an explosive charge. How could she be *happy* anywhere, under any circumstances, when she knew cancer was going to kill her in a matter of months—perhaps even days?

We pulled our chairs closer together so we could talk and hear each other above the band music. She was curious about my life and religious beliefs, even impressed that I wanted to study theology and be a pastor some day. During a lull in the conversation, I turned to focus back on her.

"Can I ask you a really personal question?"

"Sure."

"How can you be so cheerful and optimistic all the time when you know . . . I mean, when you *don't* know from one day to the next what the future holds for you?"

Her lips tightened and she looked away quickly, her eyes suddenly filling with tears. "I do feel bitter and angry at times," she finally admitted in a soft voice. "When I was a little girl I used to dream about what it would be like when I grew up. What kind of man would I marry? What would our children be like? Where would my life take me?"

"Please forgive my crass stupidity, Mary Ann. I didn't mean to make you feel sad."

She struggled to smile and nodded. "I know you didn't, and you haven't. Your question just caught me by surprise. Most people treat me like I was a fragile china doll that might break any second. Would you believe, nobody has ever once asked me how I felt about all this? Last week I overheard a friend tell my mother, 'You shouldn't talk about this around her. She doesn't need to think about it.' "

We looked at one another and burst out laughing. Did people really think she'd *forget* her circumstances if they didn't talk about it around her?

"I guess we're all afraid of being inadequate in the face of another's pain and suffering," I admitted. "If we don't talk about it, maybe it will go away."

She looked at me thoughtfully for a moment before going on. "Do you know the story in Daniel, about the three guys who were cast into a fiery furnace and how they were saved?"

Startled, I nodded. Did she think God might heal her, granting her a last-minute reprieve from her death sentence?

"No, I don't think God is likely to wave a magic wand and

cure me," she laughed, reading my face. "It's possible, and I pray for that healing. But I don't have any reason to think it might happen."

"He might if . . ."

She shook her head and pressed her finger against my lips. "He might, but He's already saved me *in the flames*." She could tell from my confusion that I didn't understand.

"You can take a lot of heat when you know for sure that God loves you, that He is with you in whatever furnace you find yourself," she said softly. "The fire doesn't destroy you; it just burns away the ropes that tie you up in knots—ropes of fear, despair, and hopelessness."

She turned to watch the couples dancing. I studied her in silence for the next few minutes, thinking she was even more beautiful than before. Although my faith's tradition disapproves of dancing, I decided this wasn't the time to split fine hairs. I stood up and held my arms out to her. "Mary Ann, I don't know anything about dancing. But if you're willing to risk your toes and teach me a bit, let's try it."

This was my first *personal* encounter with human suffering. I'd read stories about missionary doctors and nurses trying to heal disease and suffering in far-off places, but they were a distant abstraction that I couldn't relate to at age eighteen. Even though my father had died suddenly when I was a child, it was so long ago, I barely remembered the event and had no context within which to think about the unfairness of his untimely death at age twenty-nine.

But Mary Ann wasn't an abstraction. She was a warm, lovely young woman, gaily dancing in my arms. Yet a lethal disease was slowly stealing away her life even as we danced. It was so terribly unfair and surreal. How could she be so profoundly happy and at peace with what was happening in her young life? I didn't understand it then.

Like Moses before the burning bush, I knew I was standing in the presence of a holy mystery. This mystery—the human ability not only to endure suffering with such graceful trust and faith in God, but to actually transcend circumstances of suffering—perplexed me for years.

Mary Ann died a few months later, much wiser than her years. I wouldn't discover this wisdom for myself until two decades later, when painful circumstances crashed in upon my own life. Fortunately, Mary Ann left me with something special to think about: a memory of courage and faith in God, and the wisdom that goes with *acting* on that faith.

To *be* like Christ in this world may mean sharing in His suffering, and that's a lot easier to talk about than to live. But those who accept the experience make a wonderful discovery: Opening our lives up to God's transforming power in the midst of adversity radically transforms our lives and the way in which we affect the quality of life and faith of other people.

When I think of all the people I've known over the years who were trapped in a variety of painful circumstances, I have to admit that the most profoundly Christ-like people are those who have suffered deeply. They are living witnesses to the goodness of God, even in the fiery furnace of adversity. From their *burning*, light pours forth, illuminating a spiritual path through the darkness for the rest of us.

The German theologian Jurgen Moltmann says we need more people who are willing to share in Christ's suffering, to be living witnesses to God's redemptive grace in modern life. "It seems to me that today we need people who are prepared to enter into the inner wilderness of the soul and wander through the abysses of the self in order to fight with demons, and to experience Christ's victory there; or simply in order to make an inner space for living possible, and to open up a way of escape for other people through spiritual experience. And in our context this means: Wresting a positive meaning from the loneliness, the silence, the inner emptiness, the suffering, the poverty, the spiritual dryness."

His prescription is a challenge to every Christian who takes discipleship to Christ seriously—no matter what his circumstances. But the only way to *be* like Christ is to *follow* Christ and *do* what He did as He outlines in His first sermon: "The Spirit of the Lord is upon me; he has appointed me to preach Good News to the poor; he has sent me to heal the broken-hearted and to announce that captives shall be released and the blind shall see, that the downtrodden shall be freed from their oppressors, and that God is ready to give blessings to all who come to him" (Luke 4:18, 19, TLB).

To accept that mission as our own, whether we live in a

palace or a prison of the most painful circumstances, will transform our lives and those of the people we touch.

I'm sorry I never got to thank Mary Ann for what she shared with me, but this book is a start. I began organizing my thoughts and experiences on January 1, 1988, a month after the Tennessee parole board refused to hear my petition for a commutation of sentence. I'd been in prison for ten years, convicted of a murder I didn't commit, and sentenced to a ninety-nine-year prison term. "I don't know how you even keep your sanity, much less your faith, after all these years," a friend said at the time. "I know you must feel bitterly hurt and betrayed. How do you keep going on?"

How, indeed? There are days when I don't think I've got enough energy or courage to get out of bed in the morning and go at it anymore. But I've discovered something beyond the pain and unfairness: God's infinite love and presence *in the flames* with me. As Job learned during his own ordeal of suffering, that's enough.

The Key to Freedom is my attempt to explore the mystery of human faith when cast into flames of bitter suffering. My own experience—and those of close friends suffering in a wide variety of painful circumstances—forced me to ask the hard questions: Why do people suffer in a world created by a loving, perfect, all-powerful God? How does a Christian find a faith-filled path beyond prison walls of what often appears to be irrational and unfair suffering?

The following chapters were first published as a series of articles in the prison newspaper under my monthly column. Most of the chapters have since been published as separate articles in a variety of Christian magazines. Although I call upon my own experience behind literal prison walls, this book is not primarily about penitentiary life. Prison is merely the arena within which I've explored the questions.

I hope some of the experiences from my own life, and those of others described in this book, will help you find a secure and faith-filled path to follow when the days and nights of your own life turn stormy.

Jeris E. Bragan
January 1, 1990

One

When You Walk Through a Storm

The heavy steel door slammed shut behind me. For the first time, I heard the lock click behind me on Thursday, September 15, 1977, at 8:45 p.m. It's a memorable sound! I walked across the cell toward the bars, straining to look out over the dark city skyline I knew so well.

As I looked out at a world framed by prison bars, the chilling words of Judge Joseph F. Dirisio still echoed in my mind: "Jeris E. Bragan, on the verdict of the jury finding you guilty of murder in the first degree, it is the judgment of the court that you are guilty of that offense. You are sentenced, therefore, to ninety-nine years in the state penitentiary."

With the swift stroke of a judicial pen my life was changed forever. But there was one ugly flaw in this smooth administration of justice: *I wasn't guilty!*

Life can be brutally unfair.

Torrential rain swept in over the city. Lightning ripped and slashed like a flaming saber through the night sky. Bone-rattling thunderclaps shook the building that held me, while a

17

furious wind slapped sheets of water against the window. But the raging storm outside was small compared with the tumultuous storm swirling within me.

After two weeks of a bitterly contested murder trial, I was held within the cold, unforgiving arms of my worst nightmare: *prison!* I shook the bars in my cell, unconsciously trying to break the steel loose, until the blood drained from my fingers, and they turned as numb as the rest of me felt.

Another prisoner working as a trustee on the catwalk stopped by the bars and peered in, looking at me curiously as he slowly swept the concrete floor. "They've gotcha on a suicide watch, you know," he whispered furtively. Then he tapped the bars near my head. "The last dude in this cell was a seventeen-year-old kid. He hung hisself right from these bars."

"Why do they have *me* on a suicide watch?" I asked.

He shrugged. "Who knows why they do anything?" he muttered as he looked at the gold watch and wedding band on my right hand. "You wanna sell 'em?" he asked, jerking his thumb at the jewelry. "I'll give 'ya ten bucks or a couple nickel sacks of weed for 'em."

He walked away, whistling cheerfully when I declined his offer, and I was left alone again with my thoughts. Emotionally and physically exhausted, I slipped to my knees and wept. "God, *why* would You let this happen!" I muttered bitterly.

My melancholy introspection was interrupted an hour later when I heard a radio playing softly from a cell farther down the catwalk. The song sounded vaguely familiar, but I couldn't make out the words at first over the roar of thunder. Then the storm suddenly went silent, and the music seemed to fill my cell:

> When you walk through a storm,
> Hold your head up high,
> And don't be afraid of the dark.
> At the end of a storm
> Is a golden sky
> And the sweet silver song of a lark.
> Walk on through the wind—
> Walk on through the rain—
> Though your dreams be tossed and blown.

Walk on, walk on, with hope in your heart,
And you'll never walk alone.
You'll never walk alone.

The lyrics kept playing over and over in my mind, even after the music stopped. I could hear my Aunt Marion Harris singing that song as she used to do when I was a child attending an old country church in Norridgewock, Maine. I didn't realize it that night, but that encouraging song would come back to me again and again in the coming years as other storms rolled over me.

But at that moment I felt indescribably alone and abandoned.

There is enough pain and suffering in human existence to leave us wondering at times if life is anything more than a cruel joke. Sooner or later, everyone feels the biting sting from the lash of suffering. A career is demolished on the rocks of vicious gossip. A relationship is sabotaged by betrayal. Financial security crumbles in debt and ruin. Health is crippled by disease. Vibrant life vanishes, swallowed up in death.

We all ask the Why questions when our souls are ravaged by grief and anguish. I asked the questions in a thousand ways for months after my conviction—thoughtfully, at times, and at other times in smoldering anger, bitterness, and self-pity.

From my prison cell I read the biblical story of Joseph with a fresh perspective. It's a powerful story, well worth the forty-five minutes it will take for you to read it at your leisure. After reflecting on Joseph's ordeal I began to come to terms with my own storms.

Briefly, Joseph was a pampered rich kid, sold into Egyptian slavery at age seventeen by jealous brothers. While enslaved to Potiphar, his suffering was made worse when Potiphar's wife tried to seduce him. Although he sidestepped her seduction, she accused him of rape and he was flung into prison. Alone and apparently abandoned, he lingered in prison for years. But dramatic events suddenly brought about his release. The Pharaoh appointed him prime minister, and eventually, during a worldwide famine, he was reunited with his brothers and father.

Because we know the story has a happy ending, there's a

temptation to breeze lightly through the drama, oblivious to the shocking brutality, humiliation, and despair this young man endured during his thirteen-year imprisonment.

Whether ancient or modern, suffering drives us to ask some hard questions: Why do people suffer unjustly in a world created by a good, perfect, all-powerful God? It's an important question that we'll explore later in this book.

But the story of Joseph—and my memory of Mary Ann from years before—led me to focus on the issue of suffering from a slightly different perspective: *How* do we, like Joseph, begin life again when our freedom, relationships, hopes, finances, or health are seized in the cruel jaws of suffering? *How* do we cope? *How* do we find a path beyond?

You may never live in a prison made of steel like Joseph's or mine. But a wheelchair, a broken marriage, a hospital bed, poverty, abandonment—all these and many other kinds of victimization are very real prisons. They're every bit as confining, isolating, and bruising as dungeons made of steel.

As I write, I begin my thirteenth year behind prison walls. There have been many difficult and painful days. Although occasional glimmers of hope for release break through every once in a while, the ninety-nine-year sentence grinds on.

Yet I've never been more free in my life!

While trapped behind prison walls I've discovered in my study of the Bible—particularly in the story of Joseph—five keys to freedom, which lead to release and renewal beyond suffering. No matter who you are or what your circumstances may be, you too can use these keys when you walk through a storm of suffering.

1. Key to freedom in faith

For most people, faith in a loving, gracious God is challenged most violently in the bitter acid of suffering. Faith is easy during the "days of wine and roses," when we're surrounded on all sides by family, loving friends, success, and prosperity. But what does faith mean when everything we've ever loved and believed in suddenly crumbles in ashes?

Clarance Jordon answers the question with penetrating insight in his paraphrase of Hebrews 11:1: "Now faith is the turning of dreams into deeds. It is betting your life on the unseen realities, and by so relating our lives we become aware that history is woven to God's design."

Knowing that our individual histories are "woven to God's design" is the beginning of a mature, adult faith. That doesn't mean God is going to magically "fix" our painful circumstances by changing them to something more desirable. But it does mean that no matter what happens or how things appear at any given moment, our lives are *still* "woven to God's design."

From age seventeen to thirty Joseph was put through the proverbial meat grinder. Whatever could go wrong, did! Yet two astonishing themes dominate his story during those dark and difficult days. One is implicit throughout the story: his uncompromising faith in God. The second is spelled out clearly: "While Joseph was there in the prison, the Lord was with him" (Genesis 39:20, 21).

During those grim days of loss and anguish, Joseph had no idea what the future held for him from one day to the next. From his prison cell he didn't know the day would come when he'd see God's grace turn all the evil he had endured into good (see Genesis 45:7; 50:20). But his faith freed him even while he was in prison, because he knew by faith that God held his future securely in His hands. His life was "woven to God's design."

Faith is the God-shaped lens through which we filter and then interpret the events of life. Through the eyes of faith we find meaning in our circumstances. Faith gives us the vision to see possibilities for grace in the midst of the bitterest pain, and then it gives us the courage to act in our circumstances. Faith frees us to create cosmos out of chaos, to transform stumbling blocks into steppingstones.

A friend gave me her working definition of faith. It's based on the letters of the word itself as an acronym. F-A-I-T-H: **F**or **A**ll **I** **T**rust **H**im. That kind of faith, however, can't be conjured up from the imagination by wishful thinking. It evolves as the byproduct of an ongoing, personal relationship with God such as Joseph had. Faith may emerge as a new thing in the midst of life's storms, but life is a lot sweeter during the hard times when a person has already established a mature faith in God before the storm strikes.

One of the things I've discovered about faith in my thirteen years of imprisonment is this: Suffering doesn't weaken or strengthen our faith. It merely measures our *will* to exercise faith and our *capacity* for faith.

Joseph's treatment was grossly unfair. He suffered deeply through no fault of his own. But his predicament had nothing to do with whether he kept his faith in God or threw it away. The shocking abuse he endured was simply an *occasion* in which he was free to choose, as he pleased, either faith and trust in God or despair, hopelessness, and cynicism.

Faith is the first key to opening the door of imprisonment in suffering, because it opens our eyes to God's gracious action on our behalf. Even in the midst of excruciating pain, that vision of reality gives us courage and hope. It renews our energy and enthusiasm.

2. Key to freedom in acceptance

A woman went to her pastor for counseling after suffering a long series of painful experiences. Caught in the web of suffering, she kept asking the classic Why questions. Nothing her pastor said could get her to take one step beyond her pain.

Finally, he resorted to some tough love. "Tell me something," he said one day, "what's so special about you that you thought you'd get through life without any real suffering?"

Stunned, the woman angrily stormed out of his office, calling him everything but an ordained member of the clergy! After some reflection, however, she realized he wasn't being cruel. He wanted her to face the fact that life has rough edges and *nobody* is exempt from pain.

We all hurt, and we make life more difficult for ourselves by refusing to come to terms with things that can't be changed.

Johnny West, a prisoner sentenced to ninety-nine years for the killing of a Memphis, Tennessee, policeman, flatly refused to accept his circumstances. Every day of his life in prison—for twenty-three years!—he bitterly protested his innocence to anybody who would listen. Little else occupied his time, interest, or attention. Obsessed with the injustice he suffered, he nursed and rehearsed his wounds daily, keeping them fresh and sore.

The years passed. He grew more sour, and then his health failed. His family and friends died off. New friends avoided him because he was so depressing to be around. For twenty-three years he put living, loving, and laughing on hold—and then it was gone. A broken and bitter man, he died six months after he was paroled.

Frankly, I believe he was wrongly convicted. But what good did all that anger do him? The prayer of St. Francis of Assisi would have done him more good: "Lord, grant me the courage to change the things I can, the patience to accept the things I cannot change, and the wisdom to know the difference."

A faithful person can accept suffering without lingering bitterness because he knows that when God leads us into suffering, it is to stretch us, to enlarge us to receive more of His gifts of grace. Without the lens of faith to filter all the random and destructive events of life, however, we're left blind to God's saving action in our lives.

Who could have blamed Joseph if, like Johnny West, he had tried to escape or had surrendered his life to bitterness and hostility? How different life would be today if he had. Egypt, the cradle of Western civilization, would have been destroyed by a famine. Joseph's family would have perished. No Moses. No Exodus. No Israel.

Faith freed Joseph to accept his difficult circumstances. And today, four thousand years later, our individual lives are different because a young man acted on his faith in God's providential care and accepted his circumstances with grace and courage.

Accepting our situation doesn't mean we enjoy it because, like bitter medicine, it's somehow "good" for us. Who wants to die of cancer, lose a child to drowning, or be unjustly imprisoned? Only a masochist enjoys pain! But there comes a time when we have to accept "what is" as unchangeable—at least for the moment.

The dead are gone. Degenerative disease can't be reversed. An estranged spouse isn't coming home again. And prison doors won't open for me just because that's what I want.

Accepting our circumstances means putting a period at the end of the sentence. This is the second key to freedom. It allows us to get on with life again when the time for grieving has passed.

3. Key to freedom in attitude

A major-league baseball umpire had a reputation for taking his time when calling a pitch behind the plate. Seconds would tick off before he bellowed, "Ball!" or "Strike!"

The manager of a losing team finally exploded one day as the delays got longer. He stormed from the dugout, livid and screaming, "Are you blind? Don't you know the difference between a ball and a strike?"

The umpire glared at the furious manager. "It ain't *nothin'* until I call it *somethin'!*" he roared.

When I came to prison, I lost everything: my freedom, reputation, property, friends. Or so it seemed at first. Each new day was a blistering reminder of what had been taken away, leaving me a *nonperson* with a number stenciled on my back. That was a paralyzing confrontation with personal powerlessness.

Those feelings were hammered like a spike through my soul one day when a particularly vicious and sadistic jailer walked up to me while I was talking on the telephone. Without warning, he jerked the phone out of my hand and slammed it down on the receiver.

"What are you doing?" I shouted, struggling to control my anger. He thrust his mottled face close to mine. The sour smell of alcohol and tobacco blasted my nostrils.

"You ain't nothin' anymore, Bragan!" he hissed. "You're just another stinkin' convict, and I'll rip your [expletive deleted] head off if you ever give me any trouble."

He cursed me in the most colorful terms, baiting me, challenging me to respond to his malicious provocation. Other prisoners stood nearby, snickering, watching in amusement, anxious for a fight. My fists balled. Blood pounded like bass drums in my skull. I wanted to slam this grotesque human being against the wall.

Suddenly, in a microsecond of time, I experienced one of those rare, almost blinding flashes of spiritual illumination. I realized that everything, including my life, could be taken away from me in this demented, demonic, and deadly place— except for one thing. *Nothing could take away my freedom to choose how I responded to what happened to me.*

"It ain't nothin' until I call it somethin'." That realization lanced the boil of my anger. I turned and walked away.

Recognizing this level of freedom is both exhilarating and unnerving. The joy comes in confronting radically new and exciting possibilities. At least we own our feelings and can choose how we respond, regardless of circumstances. We can refuse to dance in anger or self-pity on the puppet strings of external provocation.

But real freedom can be scary because of the responsibility that comes with it. Gone are all the excuses. We no longer have anybody to blame for how we feel. Our response to all of life's blessings or blisters is ours to do with as we please.

It ain't nothin' until I call it somethin' is the way Joseph lived. He wasn't willing to squander precious energy on resentment, anger, or self-pity. Instead, he focused on what he had left.

That key opens the prison door another crack.

4. Key to freedom in action

Millions of people enjoyed George Peppard's TV portrayal of Colonel Hanibal Smith on "The A Team." Each week he and his team, consisting of B.A., Murdock, and Face, were trapped by adversaries in an impossible situation. Just when things looked most hopeless, Hanibal would always look around and begin to grin. "Don't you just love it when a plan comes together?" he would say.

The others, well aware of their peril, would always be astonished and exasperated by Hanibal's glee. They didn't immediately see why he was so exuberant. But where they saw piles of useless junk—old pipes, bags of fertilizer, a broken-down truck, and rolls of wire—he saw all the raw material to build tools, weapons, and a means of escape. In short order, under Hanibal's leadership, team members forgot their deadly circumstances and got to work with whatever resources were available to them.

"People who say it can't be done are always being interrupted by somebody doing it," my father used to say. Possibilities for success and achievement exist in the midst of the worst problems.

While thumbing through my Bible in the jail, a phrase

caught my eye: "What are you doing here, Elijah?" (1 Kings 19:9). That question nagged me for days. What *can* I do here? I wondered. I couldn't see beyond the isolation and hopelessness.

Then Margaret Sharp, an elderly friend, came to visit me. "Well, what are you gonna do here, boy?" she asked.

"You've gotta be kidding," I snapped irritably. "What am I supposed to do in a place like this?"

A person who loved me less might have indulged my self-pity. Not Margaret. She'd overcome too many obstacles in her own life to tolerate self-indulgent bitterness.

"You can do anything you want," she said bluntly. "Why don't you use some of that intelligence you've got and finish college? You've got time to read, study, and think. I've seen your writing, so get to work and *write!*"

In less than five minutes she ticked off enough work to keep me busy for the next twelve years. "Whatsoever your hand finds to do, do it with all your might," she added, quoting Ecclesiastes 9:10.

Although it took several years for me to sort through the rubble of my life, eventually I followed her advice. Since then I've read hundreds of books, finished a B.A. degree, published two books (plus this one) and scores of articles, and begun the process of earning an M.A. degree in pastoral counseling—all from behind prison walls. Right now, achieving that degree looks impossible, but resurrection morning teaches a Christian that through faith all things are possible and everything is subject to change.

I didn't persist with any of these goals because I enjoyed the process or because it was easy; I did it because I needed to *do something* to shake off the gloomy, suffocating shackles of meaninglessness in my life.

It wasn't easy, and I'm still in prison. But other convicts jokingly say I'm the only free world man living behind the walls. I don't feel imprisoned anymore because I focused on what I would do and then *did it*—in spite of limitations and obstacles.

Joseph's story reminds me of an old saying: "Christians are like tea bags—not worth much until they get in hot water." But it's not the hot water that matters; it's how we choose to *act* in that hot water.

Cruel suffering slammed doors of ordinary opportunity shut for Joseph. Gone was the life of wealth and privilege he'd known before. First enslaved and then imprisoned, the downward spiral made his life look hopeless.

But he didn't achieve greatness in those dismal circumstances because God waved a magic wand and made him so. No, his achievements were possible because faith energized him to accept cheerfully the painful, polishing business of growing maturity.

Whatever Joseph's hand found to do, he did it with all his dignity and might. He *acted* on the resources available. He preferred to light a candle, even a small one, than to curse the darkness. His life was blessed, and so were the lives of those he touched to this very day, when he turned the fourth key of *action* on his prison doors.

5. Key to freedom in love

Love is the fifth key, which unlocks the last door to our prison house of suffering, loss, and isolation.

The most liberated and loving people I know are those who have been deeply wounded by others. Something about being stripped to the bone, left only with raw spiritual resources for survival, leads to growth in our capacity to love.

Bob, a friend, is a tough, fiercely competitive ex-marine whose construction business was nearly wiped out in 1984 by a trusted employee who embezzled huge sums to cover gambling debts. Angry and embittered by the betrayal, Bob struggled day and night for months to overcome the devastating financial losses.

Nobody was surprised when he had the thief prosecuted and imprisoned. "I'll make him pay dearly!" he said angrily. "When I'm done with him, his own wife wouldn't spit on him if he were on fire!"

But friends were dumbfounded three years later when they learned that Bob gave financial aid to the thief's family, visited him in prison, and helped him find a new job when he got out!

"I thought you wanted to ruin him for life," I said. "Why would you do that for a person who caused you so much grief?"

A committed Christian, Bob smiled ruefully. "At first I wanted to shoot him," he admitted. "But one morning I read the words of Jesus for family devotions: ' "You have heard that it was said, 'Love your neighbor and hate your enemy.' But I tell you: Love your enemies and pray for those who persecute you" ' [Matthew 5:43, 44].

"My ten-year-old son interrupted my reading. 'Dad, does that mean we're supposed to love a man who stole from us?' he asked.

"Right then I realized that this is where the rubber meets the road in my life as a Christian. I knew God had given me loving grace and forgiven my sins. But here I was offering hatred and vengeance to a man who sinned against me. I was trapped in a worse prison than my ex-employee."

Blessed with rare wisdom, Bob—like Joseph—discovered that real love is more than convenient, self-serving sentimentality. It's an uncompromising commitment to another's growth, welfare, and happiness—his ultimate redemption. Not because he *deserves* it but because he *needs* it.

That's divine love.

Joseph's love didn't depend on how he was treated by jealous brothers, Potiphar's malicious wife, or a fellow prisoner who forgot him. He saw people as God sees them: Wounded sinners afflicted by guilt and in need of grace. His love was action-based, rooted in God's love for him, and motivated by God's command to love others. He was a living mediator of grace, and all who came near him were warmed and renewed by that loving grace.

Overcome by what he witnessed in Bob's forgiveness and desire for reconciliation, the former thief is an active Christian today who devotes many hours of his time each week to working with others who are addicted to gambling.

Bob says his own life was transformed by this experience.

"I can't explain it, but I'm much closer to people now," he says. "It's easier for me to communicate real warmth and affection to my wife, my children, and my friends."

He paused, and then smiled. "You know, love doesn't make the world go around like the song says, but it sure makes the trip worthwhile, especially during tough times."

Joseph discovered that faith is a three-letter word: *Yes.* He said *Yes* to faith in God, even when God's voice seemed silent. He said *Yes* to acceptance of his circumstances, even in the midst of apparent meaninglessness and loss. He said *Yes* to taking action, even though his opportunity for action was limited. He said *Yes* to a gracious attitude, regardless of how others acted. And he said *Yes* to love, even when confronted with malice and hatred.

While walking through the stormy years of imprisonment, I have slowly learned how to use these five keys. I won't pretend it was easy. Nothing is ever easy when your dreams are tossed and blown within the eye of an emotional and spiritual hurricane. But it got easier as I focused intently on the *How* questions first. Only then was I ready to confront the *Why* questions.

Ironically, it wasn't my confinement in prison that got me to thinking more clearly about the issue. Some deeply rooted pain in my wife's life put the issue in focus.

CHAPTER
Two

Why Does God Allow This?

When my wife, Edie, was a little girl, her mother taught her that God rewards "good" people and He punishes the "bad." Her father, who spent his life farming the rocky Maine soil, put it even more bluntly: "You reap what you sow."

In church she listened with rapt attention as she heard the biblical stories about God rescuing His people from their enemies. She particularly loved the dramatic stories of Joseph, Queen Esther, Daniel, and Ruth.

"I believed nothing bad could ever happen to me as long as I was good," Edie says of her childhood.

Theologians call this idea "moral reciprocity." That means we get what we deserve in life. It's a simple concept, one that even a child easily grasps.

Edie says those ideas were reassuring for her to believe in—until she turned six, when her father first subjected her to a pattern of grotesque sexual abuse. Since her mother wouldn't protect her, the abuse continued for another seven years until she was old enough to protect herself.

"I prayed every night, asking God to protect me," she recalls. "But my prayers went unanswered and the abuse got worse. One day my father encouraged my oldest brother to rape me. They both thought the experience was funny! Years later I was devastated again when I learned that my mother had always known what was happening during those years, but she didn't do anything to stop it.

"As a child I vividly recall wondering what I had done wrong to deserve such horrible treatment. Why did God allow this to happen to me?"

Curiously, in spite of the abuse she endured, Edie still liked the idea of moral reciprocity. It was something solid for her to believe in, to hang on to in an otherwise fragile and chaotic world. In her Bible she read, "He is able to save them to the uttermost" (Hebrews 7:25, KJV). She certainly felt like the "uttermost," and she chose to believe in the promise—even though she couldn't see how it was true for her.

Was this humiliating, degrading treatment by her father a reflection of God's will for her life?

Like most children, Edie wanted life to be fair. But she couldn't reconcile the problem of her abuse in a world created by a loving, all-powerful God. Consequently, like most abused children, she assumed that she was ugly and bad, even though she couldn't figure out how or why. That conflict remained a distant, disturbing problem that would haunt much of her adult life.

As she grew up it became increasingly apparent that life wasn't nearly as fair or as equitable for other people as she wanted to believe. Innocent people suffered terribly. Newspaper headlines screamed of human tragedy in earthquakes, tornadoes, floods, and famines.

"I heard these events described as 'acts of God,' " Edie says.

Then she watched an eight-year-old classmate die slowly and painfully of a malignant brain tumor. She heard about the twenty-two-year-old bride who was tortured, raped, and beaten to death by a man who broke into her home.

"A pastor told me these unfathomable events were part of the 'mystery of God's will,' " Edie says. "Even though I was distinctly uncomfortable with that bland evasion of my question, I had no satisfactory answer for my own growing list of Why questions."

At age thirty-nine, however, whatever naïve certainty she retained about moral reciprocity was forever demolished on a hot August day when she entered the Holocaust Memorial in Jerusalem. "As I moved from room to room I felt as though I'd entered hell's darkest cellar," she said about surveying evidence of the monstrous, malignant evil that had been perpetrated on the Jews during the dark days of Nazi domination in Europe. While standing at the pillar commemorating the slaughter of 1.5 million children, her stomach churned violently as she thought of her own four children.

Back on the tour bus, a friend turned her ashen face toward Edie. "How do you explain God's will in the midst of such evil? *How could God allow this to happen?*" her friend cried through clenched teeth as tears trickled down her face.

Too stunned by the horror she'd witnessed to even think of a reply, Edie could only shake her head. "Suddenly, all the easy, glib answers I'd always accepted tasted like dust in my mouth," she admits.

The problem of God's will

How could God allow such evil to happen? That is the number-one question Christians ask. College sophomores in dormitory rap sessions ask it. Theologians searching for truth ask it. And so do we all when life tumbles in upon us.

The book of Job centers on this question with great poignancy. Why is this just man subjected to such a nightmare of suffering? What has he done wrong to deserve this? It is the oldest of human questions, and for centuries men and women have struggled to find a meaningful answer.

One Christian I know answers the question with chilling clarity: "It's really quite simple. God allows evil to exist to punish people who do wrong. If we suffer, it's because we have sinned. When we see other people suffering, it's because of their sin—even though they aren't always honest enough to admit it."

What do you think of that answer?

Before exploring this question of God's will and what He allows, we need to put the issue in perspective.

First, the Why question almost always centers around *unjust* suffering. We're rarely troubled to ask why God permits something good to happen to bad people. For some peculiar reason, an "act of God" is always a flood or tornado, never a playful puppy or a moist kiss from a child.

Second, our deeply rooted adolescent beliefs about moral reciprocity create an overwhelming sense of anxiety and guilt when we ask the question within the context of our own experience. Since we've all sinned, we assume we probably deserve pain for some real or imagined guilt on our part.

It's astonishing that Christians who believe in a God of love could adopt such beliefs as part of an orthodox faith. We can only imagine the kind of guilt and anxiety an abused child must experience when he hears this kind of explanation for his victimization.

Even though the book of Job sought to refute this cruel idea centuries before Christ, it still persisted in Jesus' day. When His disciples passed a man who had been blind since birth, they asked Jesus, "Rabbi, who sinned, this man or his parents, that he was born blind?"

"Neither this man nor his parents sinned," Jesus replied, "but this happened so that the work of God might be displayed in his life" (John 9:2, 3).

In spite of what Jesus said, however, many Christians still believe the assumption behind the disciples' question.

Clearly, we have to accept responsibility for our behavior. But the Bible flatly rejects the unqualified notion that all suffering results from some specific sin we've committed. So what we must look for is an approach to the question that is biblically sound and addresses the reality of human existence as we know it.

The English theologian Leslie Weatherhead has suggested that we should think of God's will in three ways: His *intentional* will, His *circumstantial* will, and His *ultimate* will. Our common use of the phrase "The will of God" covers all three, and that creates confusion. But when we break down our understanding of God's will into these three distinctive dynamics, then the answer to our question about God's will in the midst of our suffering is focused quite clearly.

1. God's intentional will

God's intentional will for us can be seen most dramatically in the Creation story. He created an extraordinary paradise within which our first parents were to thrive and flourish. "God saw all that he had made, and it was very good" (Genesis 1:31).

The psalmist gives another clear picture of what God intended in His creation of people: "You made him a little lower than the heavenly beings [or God] and crowned him with glory and honor. You made him ruler over the works of your hands; you put everything under his feet" (Psalm 8:5, 6).

Edie has four children by a previous marriage. The youngest is now seventeen. "I looked forward to each of their births with indescribable hope and joy," she says. "A special room was designed for each of them. I spent countless hours getting everything ready for their arrival. And in my imagination I dreamed about their future possibilities."

Like every mother, Edie's "intentional will" for her children was that they should grow up, mature, and enjoy a rich, full life. Yet she also knew in advance that at times they would experience great pain in life, regardless of her intention for them.

God's *intentional* will for us is that we grow and find fulfillment in life. Jesus said, "I have come that they may have life, and have it to the full" (John 10:10). God's intentional will for us is an expression of His love. "It is not the will of your Father who is in heaven that one of these little ones should perish," Jesus insisted (Matthew 18:14, NKJV).

Yet in spite of God's intentional will, we still suffer—often unjustly—and we die. Why does God's intentional will appear to be so often thwarted? To answer that question, we have to consider God's circumstantial will.

2. God's circumstantial will

Human freedom is the operative word in understanding God's circumstantial will.

Regardless of what we intend for our children, there is a point at which we cannot protect them from the consequences of their own folly, the malice or indifference of others, or accidents. At least, we can't do that and permit their freedom.

The most loving parents must—out of love—permit their

child to suffer pain under some circumstances. We hold our children in our arms when they are given shots. We permit a baby to stumble and fall again and again as he learns to walk. How many of us have forced ourselves to walk away from our wailing child on the first day of school?

It is not our *intent* that the child suffer. But our *circumstantial* will permits it for his own good.

Most simply put, God permits evil because it is the price of our freedom. If my daughter Tracie lived eighty years in the crib where I placed her at birth, she would be protected from most of the evil in this world. She would experience few of the pains of striking out on her own. She would never stumble, but she would never walk, either.

Another dimension of God's circumstantial will strikes close to home for all of us: We are responsible and accountable to one another.

When God asked Cain, " 'Where is your brother?' " the first murderer replied, " 'I don't know. Am I my brother's keeper?' " (Genesis 4:9). In spite of Cain's cavalier indifference, we live in a community with one another, and we are mutually interdependent. What each of us does—or refuses to do—affects others. Consequently, the greatest human suffering is not caused by what *God* allows but by what *we* allow as a result of our willful ignorance, benign neglect and indifference, or outright malice.

We, not God, are accountable—individually and collectively—for events like the Holocaust. *We* are responsible when massive famine and starvation sweep over the lands, when individuals and families are driven from their homes into the streets by poverty, when greed fuels inflation and interest rates. God gives us the freedom to act ethically and morally on these responsibilities, or to refuse them as Cain did. Either way, the choice is ours. And God holds us accountable for the consequences of what we do or don't do (see Matthew 25:31-46).

The price of our freedom is the risk of evil, of sin, of pain. They come together, as a package. Whether it's a good deal or not, each has to decide for himself whether to accept it. And whatever our package holds, it's the only one we have.

If God did not give us freedom as our highest gift, then

35

there would be no circumstantial will to consider, because there would be no circumstance outside of His intent. But God gives us freedom to choose, to make mistakes and fail, to struggle.

So we speak of God's circumstantial will as what He permits, given the circumstances in which we, in our freedom, find ourselves.

3. God's ultimate will

A friend of mine, a single mother, was having serious problems with her teenage son. He had put her in a position where she had to exercise some tough love and banish him from the house to live with another family, where the father made him toe the mark and show respect for other people—especially his mother.

Feeling bitter and rejected, the boy was convinced for months that his mother had abandoned him and didn't want anything more to do with him. He didn't know that she cried herself to sleep every night because she missed him and felt so bad for him.

In fact, her ultimate will was that he come to terms with mature responsibility and be reconciled with the family. She loved him so much that she was willing to risk the loss of his love by putting him into a position—admittedly a painful one—where he had to think about the consequences of his behavior.

Within a year he grew up considerably. Today, she's closer to that son than she ever dared hope.

By the way in which we individually or collectively exercise our freedom, we may hinder or even divert God's purposes temporarily. The angel Gabriel, for example, was hindered by the prince of Persia from coming to Daniel's aid for twenty-two days (see Daniel 10:13).

But God's *ultimate* will is the redemption of His people, and His will *will* be done. Nothing can thwart God's redemptive will, ultimately. It is the direction of all human history.

From beginning to end, the New Testament throbs with the promise of redemption for those who accept Christ as their Saviour. As John 3:16 so poignantly reveals, God passionately and personally put Himself on the line to achieve His ultimate will—the redemption of His people. " 'Do not let your hearts be troubled,' " Jesus told His disciples shortly before His execution. " 'Trust in God; trust also in me. . . . I am going . . . to prepare a place for you. And if I go and prepare a place for you, I will come back and take you to be with me' " (John 14:1-3).

Moments after Jesus ascended into heaven, angels told the witnesses, " 'Why do you stand here looking into the sky? This same Jesus, who has been taken from you into heaven, will come back in the same way you have seen him go into heaven' " (Acts 1:11).

That's the ultimate promise for every Christian.

We're not alone

Meanwhile, whatever approach we take to understanding the problem of our suffering in the world, one central fact remains: *We are not alone in the struggle.* Jesus speaks to us in our suffering today: "Lo, I am with you alway, even unto the end of the world" (Matthew 28:20, KJV). And "I will never leave thee, nor forsake thee" (Hebrews 13:5, KJV).

God is with us. This is true whether we are satisfied with our personal answers or not, whether life flows easily or hard for us. Suffering may be a very real part of your life right now, but so is God. He is with you, making you to lie down in green pastures, leading you beside still waters, restoring your soul. He doesn't detour you around the valley of death's dark shadow. He walks with you through it, and out again.

In writing of what God intends, permits, and plans, I don't pretend to have solved the theological riddle about suffering that has disturbed the serenity of Christian people for centuries. But I do hope to stir your thinking so that it won't be too thin on top when you are forced to dip into it for nourishment and strength.

The next stop on my faith journey brought me into a shocking confrontation with what God actually wills for our lives, especially when we walk through the towering storms of adversity. What does Paul mean when he says, "All things work together for good for those who love God and are willing to fit into his plans"? (Romans 8:28, author's paraphrase). How does this familiar promise agree with the three dimensions of God's will?

Three

Making Sense Out of Suffering

Wednesday morning, December 23, 1987. Nervously, I watched the minute hand crawl around the large institutional clock in the prison school. Convict students and staff teachers were having a Christmas party, but I was too tense to join them in their celebration. My mouth was far too dry for munching on Christmas cookies!

After a decade of incarceration, the parole board was finally hearing my petition for executive clemency. I felt like the sword of Damocles hung over my head.

Friends familiar with my case couldn't understand my apprehension. "You should never have been convicted in the first place," one exasperated lawyer told me. "Besides, I've never seen a more strongly documented case for wrongful conviction. And you've got the best institutional record in prison that the board has ever seen. What are you so worried about?"

Christian friends were even more emphatic. "I have this conviction that God is going to change things when you least expect it, and you'll be on your way home," one insisted.

Maybe, I thought. But I knew two of the board members had a flagrant conflict of interest where my case was concerned. I also knew that prison is a place were Murphy's law is usually the dominant principle: Whatever can go wrong, will. In any event, after witnessing ten years of the most grotesque savagery imaginable in this human zoo, including twenty-nine stabbing murders, I wasn't persuaded that God was in the business of arbitrarily interfering with the abuse people inflict on one another just for their personal convenience.

Yet, I still hoped God would answer my prayer for release.

One of the teachers poked her head into the office where I waited. "Edie is on the phone for you," she said. I took a deep breath before picking it up to hear her tell me the results of the hearing.

"I'm afraid it's bad news," she said.

"Well, that won't be an entirely new experience," I replied. "What's the verdict?"

"We lost. The vote was three to two," she said. Her voice trembled. I knew she was on the verge of tears, and I suddenly felt very tired, alone, and betrayed—again.

A familiar biblical passage kept ricocheting around like a spent bullet in the back of my mind as I walked through the prison yard toward my cellblock: "We know that all that happens to us is working for our good if we love God and are fitting into his plans" (Romans 8:28, TLB).

I shivered uncomfortably in the winter chill. More than once I'd shared that promise with friends when they struggled through hard times. But now the words tasted bitter in my mouth. The promise sounded like an empty cliché. I manifestly did *not know* and could *not see* how in all things God was working for *my* good.

I looked up at the slate-gray sky. "Thanks a lot, Lord. And merry Christmas to You too!" I muttered angrily.

In spite of my feelings, I walked up to the prison chapel later that night to celebrate Christmas Mass. Although I am Seventh-day Adventist, I've always appreciated Father Ralph, the sisters, and Catholic laypeople who volunteer their time at the prison. Moreover, because we're small in number, Christian brothers from different traditions tend to support one another's faith in prison. We share open communion, regardless of which faith community a prisoner is connected with.

The congregation was standing for prayer as I stepped into the back of the chapel. "I pray for those who were denied clemency this morning," I heard one of the men say. And the congregation responded in unison, "We pray to the Lord."

Later, tears stung my eyes as Father Ralph handed me the wafer. "The Body of Christ," he said quietly.

He knew I wasn't Catholic and that our religious traditions viewed the sacramental symbols quite differently. But none of that mattered. He knew of my discouragement, and in that moment we were just two fellow pilgrims, Christian brothers, each in need of the saving, rescuing, resurrecting grace that can be experienced most profoundly during communion.

Dr. John Mallette, an ordained deacon and a professor at Tennessee State University, presented the cup. "Be of good cheer, my friend. The Lord bless you," he said.

As I walked through the prison compound that night, I stopped and looked up at the star-studded sky. Nearly two thousand years ago Christ had put aside His divine power and glory to join us in the crucible of human uncertainty, unfairness, and suffering. I wondered if He had always been certain of God's abiding presence during rough times in His life. And then I remembered His cry of utter despair from the cross, " 'My God, my God, why have you forsaken me?' " (Matthew 27:46). Those weren't His last words, however. Faith burst forth as His life slipped away: "Jesus called out with a *loud* voice, 'Father, into your hands I commit my spirit' " (Luke 23:46).

I understood how He felt.

It was a deeply spiritual moment as I stood alone in the middle of the prison compound, surrounded on all sides by walls, barbed wire, and gun towers. There was something about the Christmas season and communion at the end of this difficult day that provoked a truly energizing moment of Epiphany for me.

During a day of great pain and restlessness, I suddenly felt a deeply rooted spiritual awareness of Christ's abiding presence in my anguish. The same problems remained; I had no idea what the future held. But in that moment I felt mysteriously *resurrected*, more confident about whatever came next in my life. I felt energized with hope and courage, even though both seemed either pointless or silly under the circumstances.

The experience was something beyond words or logic. I could accept or reject the offer of grace, but I could not analyze it. Like Job, I didn't have an intellectual answer to my questions; I had something far more transcending—God's presence. That was good enough for the moment. "Thank You, Lord, for trusting me with this," I prayed as I headed toward my cell.

A restless ex-detective

The drudgery of prison life closed around me again as the weeks passed, smothering that fleeting glimpse of God's grace on the prison compound. And then came the hard, pounding questions about the reality of faith in God.

Only a person with religious faith is driven to ask the ultimate Why questions about meaning in the midst of suffering. This is true because we worship a loving, gracious, and omnipotent God, and the problem of evil in the midst of a world created by such a God is a baffling mystery.

There is no mystery about suffering for the irreligious person. To him, evil is a relative value judgment. He views life as little more than an endless battle between the small and weak who struggle for survival against the large and powerful in a brutal, bloody, ruthless food chain of eaters and the eaten. Survival of the fittest is the only ethical law.

Consequently, in an increasingly irreligious world, where everything is so relative that nothing is related, the biblical assurance of Romans 8:28 sounds like an absurd proposition, a religious relic from a bygone superstitious age, something for the naïve to hang on to when they need to make sense out of nonsense.

For a person of faith, however, it is during times of great suffering that our glittering religious assumptions are challenged most bitterly. At such times we remember the sermons we've heard about how God answers prayer; we remember the magnificent stories about people in the Bible facing incomprehensible ordeals and how God delivered them. Within the cloistered security of a church pew, we see with crystal clarity how "in all things God works for the good of those who love him" (Romans 8:28).

But what do we say of our own concrete circumstances?

When you were fired from your job, denied the promotion you deserved because of race or gender, suffered from unfair and vicious gossip, were betrayed by your spouse, or watched your child drift into various addictions—were *you* confident that "in all things God works for the good" in your life? What possible good can come out of the suffering we experience in brutalizing disease, the untimely death of a child, or the awesome genocide of huge populations that has characterized this century?

These are hard, deeply personal questions that challenge our assumptions about faith in God. Glib answers won't do.

Throughout the following months I struggled with my questions. Can I know the truth of this biblical promise only through the eyes of faith? I wondered. Is it only in eternity that we'll discover the "good" in our suffering? Was I too blind or too self-centered to see the "good" in spending more years behind prison walls? Was God trying to teach me some lesson that I stubbornly refused to deal with?

And those questions led to tougher ones.

What if faith in God is all just an illusion, a silly superstition dreamed up by the pious or the fearful? What if there is no God after all? What if there is no meaning in my circumstances or anyone else's? Perhaps we don't honestly admit these questions openly to one another, but we've all confronted them—if only timidly—during times of silence in the soul when our lives spin out of control.

Although intellectual honesty compelled my questions, that same honesty forced me to acknowledge the powerful experiential existence of God's presence in my life. I *knew* God wasn't a figment of my imagination. I also *knew* the biblical promise *was* true, even if I couldn't figure out *how* it was true.

Finally, I *knew* God required both a reasonable faith and a faithful reason from me. I didn't know what the answers were to my questions. But this ex-detective wouldn't rest until the mystery was unraveled.

What is the "good" for me?

People with a mature faith in God can endure virtually any kind of suffering if they can find some way to make the experience meaningful. If we truly "know that all that happens to us is working for our good if we love God and are fitting into his plans," then what happens to us is profoundly meaningful.

But during rough times, when our lives are ripped and battered by tragic events, the deeply rooted fear that *nothing matters* haunts our lives, drowns our hopes, and drives us into the wilderness of despair.

As I explored Romans 8:28 thoughtfully, it seemed to me there were three issues to be sorted out: Did I truly love God? Was I fitting into His plan? And was there any evidence of "good" within my circumstances?

First, I knew that I loved God, just as surely as I loved my wife and children. Second, although I didn't know the specifics of His plan for my life at this point, I knew that I was willing to fit into any plan He had, and I felt confident in saying that because of the promise of Jeremiah 29:11: " 'I know the plans I have for you,' declares the Lord, 'plans to prosper you and not to harm you, plans to give you hope and a future.' "

So the first two issues weren't a problem.

But I felt stuck on the third point. Yet in spite of my restless anxiety, I couldn't ignore the compelling array of evidence that God had blessed my life in a wide variety of ways and that a lot of good had evolved from my experience. So I wrote out a list for review and reflection. When times are tough, it is an energizing experience to write out a specific list of ways in which God is blessing you.

First, I had to admit that my ten-year wilderness experience behind prison walls had given me time to study, think, and reflect on a variety of theological and philosophical issues that were important to me. The demands of free-world life would have drastically cut the time I had spent on these subjects.

Second, although I was a Christian before coming to prison, behind prison walls I've experienced the deepest fellowship with Christ, the greatest personal liberation. The German theologian Jurgen Moltmann, once a prisoner of war himself, described this mystical experience of spiritual liberty in his book *Experiences of God*: "It is not going too far to say that prison is the place where the deepest experience of Christian liberty is to be found. In prison the spiritual presence of Christ is felt."

Moltmann described my experience perfectly.

Third, in addition to uninterrupted time to think and write, this demonically evil place also provided me with a dramatic environment in which I could observe God's grace breaking through the sin-encrusted souls of men whom the rest of the world has given up on. As Paul said, "Where evil abounded, grace did much more abound" (Romans 5:20, KJV).

Fourth, I doubt that I would ever have gotten around to publishing my writing had I not come to prison. I ran a thriving, successful detective agency in the free world. I enjoyed my work and was good at it. But it left little time for reflection. Writing was on my "gonna get to it one of these days" list. In prison, at last, I had something to write about!

Fifth, during the July riots that swept over Tennessee's prison in 1985, I was present as the pent-up frustration of men confined behind these walls exploded in fury. Seven correctional officers were seized as hostages. People expected the day to end in a massive bloodbath. But working together with Christian, Muslim, and solid-con brothers, we were able to defuse the violence and secure a safe release for all the hostages. While there was enormous property damage that day, there was no people damage.

I'm glad I was there.

Finally, after a twenty-five year silence, my high-school sweetheart read some of my articles and tracked me down in prison. We were married on April 8, 1989. It would be impossible to overstate the importance of the love she brings into my life. But more on this incredible love story in another chapter.

At the risk of sounding like I'm engaging in pious boasting, I could go on with a lengthy list of specific ways in which I see how God has worked for "good" in my life in spite of these difficult circumstances. But is that *all* there is?

Something deep within me knew there was more to it, but I couldn't figure out what.

The mystery unraveled

Sometimes the clues to solving a mystery are so close that we can't see the forest for the trees. As a former detective, I knew the value of walking away from a perplexing problem for a while, leaving it alone until I could come back and look at it from a fresh perspective. Several months passed before I was ready to wrestle with the theological problems that Romans 8:28 posed in my life.

And only when I finally made the connection between Romans 8:28 and Romans 8:29 did the mystery begin to clear up for me. Read the two passages together and see how radically different is the meaning: "We know that all that happens to us is working for our good if we love God and are fitting into his plans. For [or because] from the very beginning God decided that those who came to him—and all along he knew who would—should *become like his son*, so that his Son would be the First, with many brothers" (TLB, emphasis supplied).

I read the passage scores of times before the meaning finally broke through my preconceived, egocentric notions about *how* God *should* make things work out for my good. I wanted the "good" to be on my terms. For me the "good" would be freedom from prison; vindication of my name; the right to be with my family and friends; the opportunity to work and write in a less stressful, restrictive environment. In my judgment, these things were the ultimate "good" for me.

But God sees the *ultimate* good for you and me in drastically different terms. To paraphrase the text, all things—the good, the bad, and the ugly—work together by God's grace for the *ultimate good purpose of making us like Jesus.* In other words, God works for our good in all things to make us Christlike, or "conformed to the likeness of his Son" (verse 29).

Two more years have passed since that disappointing day when the parole board denied my petition. Another Christmas season is rapidly approaching, and I begin my thirteenth year behind prison walls. But I take the promise of Romans 8:28 and 29 more seriously than ever before. I no longer see it as a syrupy invitation to a life of ease and freedom from suffering. Instead, I see the promise as a personal invitation to fellowship and ministry with the risen Christ in this bruised, lacerated, and sin-torn world.

Hans Küng, one of my favorite theologians, describes the biblical claims about God's will in precise terms: "From the first to the last page of the Bible, it is clear that God's will aims at man's well-being at all levels, aims at his definitive and comprehensive good. God's will is helpful, healing, liberating, saving will. God wills life, joy, freedom, peace, salvation, the final great happiness of man."

Küng's description became my personal experience, even in the wilderness of prison, when I began learning how to break down the barriers I'd erected to God's passion to bless me within my circumstances.

CHAPTER
Four

Breaking Barriers to Blessings

It was a crisp, wintry Maine night. Tuesday, December 8, 1959. At thirteen I'd finally worked up enough nerve to ask my fifteen-year-old girlfriend, Edie Hall, to "go steady" with me. Tell me that men don't remember important dates!

She said Yes, of course!

I adored her. I thought she was the most magnificent creature on the face of God's beautiful green earth. To this day, thirty years later, I can vividly recall the incredible collage of feelings that rushed through me the first time I felt the warmth of her hand in mine. More than once my mother tartly reminded me that Edie's hand wouldn't disappear if I stopped holding it.

I knew she was right, but we were inseparable, and I wasn't about to test the theory.

The adult world around us, however, was noticeably less than thrilled with the exclusiveness of our relationship. We both were told repeatedly that we "needed to date around" and find out what other people were like. But I loved Edie and wasn't even slightly interested in what other girls were like.

Then, in August of 1961, she suddenly broke up with me. She appeared angry and hostile. Years later I learned that her mother finally pressured her into breaking off our relationship because we were going to different schools that year. Edie wanted me to talk her out of it, but I took her anger at face value. Bewildered and hurt, I walked away.

Eventually, both the romantic and hurt feelings passed, and I simply remembered her with great nostalgic warmth and some ill-defined regrets. But I didn't see her again for nearly twenty-five years. Shortly before I went to trial in 1977, a mutual friend told me that Edie had "jumped from the frying pan into the fire" of a second marriage. But by then I was too absorbed with my own personal problems to think about it.

Seven years later, on May 6, 1984, Pastor Conn Arnold walked into the prison chapel at the Tennessee State Prison and sat down beside me. He reached into his pocket, pulled out a letter, and handed it to me. It was short, just one page. I scanned it quickly—until I came to the signature, and then I froze: *Edie!*

After reading an article I'd published about Conn's work as a volunteer prison chaplain, she wrote him to say she'd recognized my byline and wanted to find out if I was the same man she'd dated as a young girl. If so, she wanted my address.

Having Edie contact me in prison was certainly not one of the things we'd planned on doing when we were teenagers years before! For the first time in many years I felt terribly defensive and vulnerable about that number on my back. I told Conn I needed to think about it before he gave her my address. After a few days of mulling it over, however, I realized my feelings weren't appropriate. Moreover, even though nearly a quarter century had passed, deep within me I knew she wouldn't think less of me because of what had happened in my life.

So I wrote to Conn and shared some personal recollections about Edie with him. I told him he could send her my address. He did. He also sent her a copy of my letter to him!

Several months passed before I heard from her. Meanwhile,

mutual friends brought me up to date on her life. It hurt deeply to hear about the suffering she'd endured for the past twenty-two years in two very difficult marriages. I couldn't help wondering "what might have been" if things had turned out differently for us.

She came to Tennessee to visit me for the first time on February 8, 1986. Whatever lingering apprehension I had about seeing her evaporated like fog under a hot sun when she walked into the room. Although the years of heartbreak had etched some painful lines about her eyes, behind the pain, the girl I'd once known had become a beautiful adult woman. I embraced her, struggling to hold back the tears.

She moved to Nashville with her four children in July, and we were married on the prison picnic area three years later, April 8, 1989—exactly twenty-nine years, four months, and fifteen hours after I first asked her to go steady with me. I do remember dates about anything connected with Edie!

Even though I was acutely aware that God had richly blessed my life during the first seven years of my incarceration, the loneliness of prison existence was catching up with me by the time I met Edie again. Only later, when we both reviewed our separate histories and saw how God brought our paths back together again, did we realize just how wonderfully God had blessed both of us. That's when I began to grasp more fully the depth of God's passion to bless people.

God's passion to bless us

When the full impact of John 3:16 struck me in my late twenties, my heart was deeply stirred by the elegant grandeur of the text: "For God so loved the world that he gave his one and only Son, that whoever believes in him shall not perish but have eternal life."

In addition to the astonishing promise of salvation and eternal life—which is phenomenal enough—I was gripped by the depth of divine passion revealed in this classic biblical passage. That passion was something I'd missed entirely before, mostly because I'd heard the passage so many times that I'd become desensitized to the shocking content of the words.

God's passion to bless people confounds the human imagination. The Bible boldly insists that He will do anything, risk everything—including Himself—in order to bless humankind and reconcile us to Himself again as "friends" (see John 15:15).

Lavishly extravagant is the most accurate phrase to use in describing God's passion to bless people.

After asking Israel to pay a tithe to support the priestly ministry, God said: " 'Test me in this. . . . And see if I will not throw open the floodgates of heaven and pour out so much blessing that you will not have room enough for it' " (Malachi 3:10).

That's lavish!

From Genesis to Revelation the Bible throbs with evidence of God's passion to bless people with all the good gifts of life: health (Exodus 23:25), long life (Psalm 91:16), wealth (Proverbs 10:22), wisdom (Psalm 32:8), success (Philippians 4:13), peace (John 14:27). The list seems endless!

The author of Revelation is virtually tongue-tied when he attempts to describe the extraordinary splendor of heaven. The best he can do is speak of "streets of gold" and architecture studded with a rich profusion of precious gems.

Jesus' behavior and His words are no less extravagant. His life is a stunning embodiment of God's passion to bless people, especially those in dire need. He restored health and vitality to multitudes who were afflicted with disease and despair. He promised His followers "mansions" in heaven (John 14:2, KJV) and abundant life on earth (see John 10:10). Finally, He surrendered His life to those who loathed Him in order to make their reconciliation with God possible.

Extravagant divine passion!

Even nature testifies to God's extravagant passion (see Psalm 19:1-3). Anybody who has walked through a field of wild daisies, buttercups, or black-eyed Susans in summer knows of God's huge enjoyment of color, form, contour, and scent. A fiery sunset leaves the most jaded and cynical standing silent in wonder.

And when we look into the warm eyes of one who loves us, then we know something intimately personal about God's passion to bless us with the most transcending joy imaginable.

What we observe in the lives of others and in our own experience provides confirming evidence of God's passion to bless us. Even though most of us have spent some painful times "in the valley of the shadow of death" (Psalm 23:4), overwhelmed with pain and sorrow, at other times we are suddenly, acutely aware that our lives are richly blessed with God's loving grace—shocking displays of unearned, unmerited favor.

If we're honest about it, most of us have to admit that we give little serious thought to God's flow of blessings in our lives when things are going well. But when our own folly, the malice of others, or the toxic chemistry of events crashes in upon us, then we are painfully aware of our need for God's blessing.

These also are the times we're in most danger of unwittingly throwing up barriers to blessings. But we'll get to that in a moment.

Suffering, particularly when it's unfair, strikes a discordant note in the otherwise joyful music of human existence. While many are phenomenally blessed, we cannot ignore the sobering evidence of others who suffer incomprehensible deprivation—who even lack the bare essentials to sustain life.

How can we reconcile this disturbing, glaring evidence with what certainly appears to be the biblical conviction that God has a passion to bless us? Does God play favorites? Are suffering people reaping the "reward" of God's wrath for their hidden sins? Or could we be doing something, perhaps without realizing it, that throws up impenetrable barriers to blessings from God?

Before exploring the specifics of the last question, a note of caution: First, I freely admit that every scrap of evidence connected with human experience doesn't appear to support my conviction that God longs to bless us. But most of it does. Second, God does *not* play favorites. In fact, Jesus scandalized His disciples when He candidly admitted that God blesses everybody—even the proverbial "bad" people (see Matthew 5:45). And third, unlike Job's dismal comforters, who were so quick to assume that his suffering was caused by secret sin, we ought to know better. Innocent, godly people do suffer unjustly throughout their lives. But even their lives can be showered with blessings from God within the most painful circumstances—especially if they know how to avoid the following five common barriers to blessings.

1. Lack of faith

A lack of mature faith in God's will blinds us to the reality of God's loving grace—His passion to bless us at *all* times in our daily lives. Without this faith, especially when we're overwhelmed in a storm of trouble, we are left demoralized and cast adrift, without a coherent guidance system, in an angry sea of anxiety, fear, and despair.

For days back in 1975 my wife Edie struggled with her faith in God's providential care while Cheyenne, her two-year-old son, fought for life after accidentally ingesting an overdose of medication.

She begged God to heal her son.

He got weaker.

She angrily accused God of indifference.

The boy lapsed into a coma.

Finally, when it appeared he had no chance of recovery, she surrendered her boy to God with the toughest prayer of her life: "Not as I will, but thy will be done," she prayed—and meant it (see Luke 22:42). The child regained consciousness within hours and made an astonishing recovery.

Did God heal her son?

"Maybe he would have recovered anyway. I simply don't know," Edie honestly admits. "But I do know God performed an important miracle for me when He broke through all my frightened begging and angry demands with the conviction that He loved me. I knew at that moment I could trust His will for Cheyenne and me, no matter what happened."

Faith opens our eyes during times of great pain and loss to see God's saving will in our lives. But the problem for many Christians is an uncertainty over how to characterize "God's will," especially when the storms of suffering wash over our lives.

Cheyenne, now seventeen, understands this important truth about God's will. "It's easy to trust God when you *know for sure* that God only wants what is best for you," he says.

God doesn't bless us *because* we have faith; the blessings are there for us in abundance whether we recognize them or not. Faith in God's will—His passion to bless us—simply opens our eyes so we can recognize the blessings, accept them, and enjoy them. Since the stoning of Stephen, Christian saints have faced every kind of death with courage because they knew the depth of God's will to bless them. Even death is not the final word.

Faith is a nonnegotiable conviction that God's will is absolutely sovereign, no matter how things appear. Faith is rooted squarely in an intimately personal relationship with a God who reigns in our lives. And the ultimate prayer of faith is this: "Thy will be done in earth, as it is in heaven" (Matthew 6:10, KJV).

Edie says her encounter with God during the near-death of Cheyenne radically transformed her personal relationship with Him and the way she confronts adversity. "I've had to cope with other trials since," she says. "Everything doesn't work out just the way I might like. But I've never gone through a painful experience yet when I didn't eventually see evidence of God's loving will working for my good. I have experienced the greatest blessing during times of deepest tragedy."

That kind of faith throws down barriers to blessings!

2. Unresolved guilt

Unresolved guilt is a spiritual termite that steadily chews away at the foundation of our relationship with God and others. It condemns us, stripping us of the freedom and healing to be found in confession, repentance, and forgiveness. Nothing destroys healthy self-esteem faster or more thoroughly than unresolved guilt. It's one of the most stubborn barriers to blessings.

Elsie Hall, my seventy-four-year-old mother-in-law, seemed to have everything a woman her age could want: excellent health, modest but adequate and secure finances, many loving friends and family members. But on the morning of January 18, 1989, she ate a light breakfast, went to the post office, returned home—and killed herself. She wanted to die so badly that she crawled into the back of her station wagon and pressed her face down against the floor near a hole so she would inhale the carbon monoxide most efficiently. It was her third attempt in two years.

People in the community were stunned by her death. Why?

It didn't make any sense. She had everything to live for.

True. But she had one more thing in her life that only a few people knew about: grinding, relentless, brutalizing guilt because decades before she had pretended not to know that her violent and abusive husband was sexually molesting their daughter. She knew about it, but she did nothing to stop it.

She would not forgive herself. She refused to believe God could forgive a sin like hers. She was convinced that Edie despised her, in spite of overwhelming evidence to the contrary. "Nobody could love me," she insisted.

Psychiatrists tried to help with drugs. A psychologist put her in group therapy. My wife tried to assure her that the past was forgiven. I tried to persuade her of God's infinite capacity to love and forgive. She knew that was true for everybody else—but not for her.

Unresolved guilt is such a critical barrier to blessings because guilt leaves us spiritually crippled, emotionally mutilated, and intellectually confused. Guilt erects a tamper-proof barrier between us and our God-given resources for reconciliation and healing.

The Bible says, "If we confess our sins, he is faithful and just and will forgive us our sins and purify us from all unrighteousness" (1 John 1:9). Forgiveness is a free gift of grace, but it has no redemptive value whatsoever until a sinner completes the transaction by accepting the gift on faith.

In the final analysis, God has provided only two methods for dealing with guilt: Either we seek forgiveness by confession and repentance, or we hang on to the guilt, carrying the backbreaking load until we are crushed by its weight.

Elsie was surrounded by compelling evidence of God's passion to bless her, but she missed it all because she refused to accept it. Instead, she clung to her guilt as though it were a life raft rather than the deathtrap it actually was.

3. Self-destructive feelings

Surrendering the control of our lives to feelings of bitterness, resentment, anger, and self-pity is *self*-destructive because the tumultuous emotional storm unleashed by such feelings is powerful enough to drown out the still, small voice of God.

After a decade of struggling with religious doubt, my adult

conversion to Christianity came quietly at age twenty-nine during a relatively minor personal crisis. I breathed a huge sigh of relief and made plans to return to college and pick up the theological education I'd abandoned in 1966.

God was in His heaven and all was well in my world at last—for a few days.

Then a veritable avalanche of unexpected problems roared over me. When the dust finally settled two-and-a-half years later, I found myself convicted of a murder I had nothing to do with and ninety-nine years in prison to think about it.

I was not a happy man!

In short order, I became a practicing expert in self-destructive feelings. During the first couple years of imprisonment, I had enough bile in my belly to pickle a cucumber with a glance! My prayers bounced off the ceiling—or so it seemed much of the time. My faith in God was shaken to the foundations. Confidence in friends evaporated, and optimism about the future turned gloomy.

The anguish of the psalmist was my own: "My God, my God, why have you forsaken me? Why are you so far from saving me, so far from the words of my groaning? O my God, I cry out by day, but you do not answer, by night, and am not silent" (Psalm 22:1, 2).

I didn't enjoy the feelings, but they had me in a suffocating stranglehold, and I didn't know how to change them.

While reading in my cell one day, I came across some lines from Martin Luther that helped me regain some control of my feelings. "Temptations are like birds flying over our heads," he wrote. "While we can't stop them from flying over, we can prevent them from building a nest in our hair."

The truth is, we can't help the way we feel when we're suffering—at least for a while. Feeling betrayed by life and God is a predictable—although inaccurate—temptation when we experience great loss. But bitter feelings become an impenetrable barrier to blessings when we stop processing those feelings and allow them to "build a nest in our hair."

Helen Keller, left blind and deaf at age two, had so much to be angry and bitter about. Who could have blamed her if she'd surrendered her life to resentment and self-pity? But she didn't. She saw herself as incredibly blessed by God—in spite of her crippling losses. "So much has been given to me; I have no time to ponder over that which has been denied," she said.

Her words slammed through the prison walls of my thinking: *So much has been given to me!* Like her, I couldn't do anything to change my circumstances, but I was free to choose how I would respond to them. I chose to concentrate on my blessings—which, frankly, didn't take long to list at first—and to thank God for them.

The self-destructive feelings that had so badly distorted my spiritual vision for months disappeared rapidly, and I experienced a great rush of blessings from God *within* my circumstances, the most important of which was a renewed awareness of God's abiding presence in my life.

4. Disobedience

Disobedience of God's law is a guaranteed barrier to blessings. We've all observed the cause and effect relationships for people who violate health, moral, criminal, and natural laws. But the Christian has an additional law to obey: *The law of discipleship.*

Virtue may be its own reward. But prior to their conversion, Jesus' disciples were hardheaded, practical men who were beginning to grasp the cost of discipleship—and it was high! The time came when they also wanted to know what were the rewards—the blessings—of discipleship. In effect, they told Jesus, "We've left everything to follow You. Now what's in it for us?" (Matthew 19:27, paraphrased).

Jesus' response was a promise of extravagant blessing. "Everyone who has left houses or brothers or sisters or father or mother or children or fields for my sake will receive a *hundred times as much* and will inherit eternal life" (Matthew 19:29, emphasis supplied).

Each one of us, like the first disciples, is confronted with Jesus' command to "follow Me!" That's not a polite invitation. It's a *command.* An invitation suggests we might have something equally important or even better to do. A command asserts the inherent need for immediate, unqualified obedience. " 'If you love me, you will do what I command,' " Jesus said (John 14:15). But what, exactly, did Jesus "command"?

While He didn't formulate a precise set of orders, the specifics are still clear.

First, He commanded us to follow His example. "I have set you an example that you should do as I have done for you," He told his disciples on the last night of His life (John 13:15). "Now that you know these things, you will be blessed if you do them" (verse 17).

As modern-day disciples we are called to a life of love-in-action, as Jesus first announced in His inaugural sermon and then proceeded to act out in His life. "The Spirit of the Lord is on me, because he has anointed me to preach good news to the poor. He has sent me to proclaim freedom for the prisoners and recovery of sight for the blind, to release the oppressed, to proclaim the year of the Lord's favor" (Luke 4:18, 19).

For the pronoun *me* in that test, we can add our own names. As Jesus told one listener in His famous parable of the good Samaritan, "Go and do likewise" (Luke 10:37).

Second, Jesus gave another equally specific command: "A new command I give you: Love one another. As I have loved you, so you must love one another" (John 13:34). He calls each one of us to love one another in unqualified self-sacrifice, the kind of love that is unconditionally committed to the growth, welfare, fulfillment, and happiness of others—especially those most in need.

Finally, Jesus said that the basis for our blessing and final judgment before God is determined by how we treat the hidden Christ in our midst today: " ' "Come, you who are *blessed* by my father; take your inheritance, the kingdom prepared for you since the creation of the world. For I was hungry and you gave me something to eat, I was thirsty and you gave me something to drink, I was a stranger and you invited me in, I needed clothes and you clothed me, I was sick and you looked after me, I was in prison and you came to visit me." ' " " ' "Whatever you did for one of the least of these brothers of mine, *you did for me*" ' " (Matthew 25:34-36, 40, emphasis supplied).

It's deeds, not creeds, that open channels to the passionate flow of God's blessing in our lives. The happiest and most blessed people I know are those who imitate Jesus' life and practice.

5. Fear of risk

Fear of taking risks is the last great barrier to blessings, because God calls each of us—no matter what our circumstances—into a divine adventure of astonishing risk taking with Him.

For me, trapped behind grim prison walls, the risk taking God demanded seemed both reckless and foolhardy. I'd been betrayed, lied to and about, falsely accused of murder. I felt totally annihilated. Yet God commanded me:

To risk unqualified faith in Him—even in the face of apparent absurdity and meaninglessness

To risk loving others—even when confronted with malice, betrayal, and indifference

To risk forgiveness—even when exploited and abused

To risk hope—even in the midst of great personal tribulation

To risk courage—even when overwhelmed with fear

To risk joy—even in a bruising wilderness of sorrow and loss.

Jesus defined God's challenge to divine risk taking in clear terms: " 'If anyone would come after me, he must deny himself and take up his cross daily and follow me. For whoever wants to save his life will lose it, but whoever loses his life for me will save it' " (Luke 9:23, 24).

"Now there's a prescription for divine madness!" I sourly thought to myself. But I couldn't forget the words. Day and night they haunted my consciousness: *I must deny myself and take up my cross daily.* I certainly had a "cross" to carry. And unable to carry it alone, the weight drove me staggering to my knees.

But I didn't *have* to carry it alone. Jesus said, " 'Come to me, all you who are weary and burdened, and I will give you rest. Take my yoke upon you and learn from me, for I am gentle and humble in heart, and you will find rest for your souls' " (Matthew 11:28, 29).

I thought about these things for a long time. And then it was time to stop thinking and to begin *acting*—taking a risk—on what I believed to be true, even though it didn't always *feel* true. But God never asked us to feel faithful, just to *be* faithful.

Although I found the above six risks demanded of me to be quite intimidating at first, I cautiously went to work on them. They were surprisingly easy to deal with once I committed myself to the process. I was keenly aware of an increasing flow of God's blessings in my life again.

But just when I thought I had everything under control and I'd finally accepted the loneliness, isolation, and obscurity of prison, friends then confronted me with a seventh risk: Publish your writing.

I stubbornly refused. "I get enough rejection every day in here; I don't need to go looking for more," I grumbled. "Besides, who wants to read the scribbles of a man in prison?"

Margaret Sharp, my old friend and a bluntly outspoken grandma, poked a large hole in my thinly disguised fear. "It's a good thing St. Paul didn't feel so sorry for himself," she said pointedly. "God has blessed you with many gifts. One is a gift for writing about God's goodness. Now use it or lose it!"

That was six years ago. Fortunately, I didn't hold my breath waiting for the chilly-to-hostile reception I expected from editors. With few notable exceptions, what I've invariably received is warmth and interest. Since then I've received a virtual flood of blessings from God—I would never have met Edie again if I hadn't started writing!

The only real difference between people who are blessed and those who aren't is this: Blessed people are willing to risk the pain of growth that comes in shouting an empathic *Yes!* to God's call upon their lives.

But it's hard to shout that Yes unless we have a sense of real joy and happiness in our lives. Ironically, behind prison walls I've had the opportunity to study and think about the issue of human happiness from a very personal perspective. Are you happy in you own circumstances today? Do you know how to create a profoundly meaningful and happy life for yourself—no matter what your circumstances? Consider this: Happiness is an inside job!

CHAPTER
Five

Happiness Is an Inside Job

Several years before my own incarceration, I spent a cold winter afternoon at a minimum security facility for federal prisoners talking with a once-powerful judge I'd known during happier times. Convicted of bribery and extortion, he'd lost everything—family, career, reputation, wealth, power.

After exchanging some awkward pleasantries, I blurted out the question I felt most compelled to ask: Why?

Thoughtfully, he stared out over the landscape before answering. "I wanted to be happy, and I doggedly pursued that goal, searching for it in success, money, power, sex, and alcohol," the former jurist said. "I got it all too." He paused. "But do you know what I really had when I 'had it all'?" he asked.

I shook my head.

He cupped his palms and held them out toward me. "Nothing but emptiness. In prison I realized that the pursuit of happiness as a goal ends in despair and meaninglessness— soul misery!"

Carl Jung, one of the great thinkers of this century, recognized this description of unhappiness decades ago: "About a third of my cases are suffering from no clinically definable neurosis, but from the senselessness and emptiness of their lives," he wrote.

Soul misery, the devastating byproduct of a meaningless life, is a modern plague that destroys the quality of life for millions. Unable to find any happiness, these people lead what Thoreau described as "lives of quiet desperation." It's the desperation people feel when they know their lives add up to nothing. That haunting realization chills any possibility for happiness, regardless of fame, wealth, or material possessions.

Said Leo Rosten, "The purpose of life is not to be happy but to matter, to be productive, to be useful, to have it make a difference that you lived at all."

Rabbi Harold Kushner agrees: "What frustrates us and robs our lives of joy is this absence of meaning. Our lives go on day after day. They may be successful, full of pleasure, or full of worry. But do they *mean* anything? Would our disappearance leave the world poorer or just less crowded?"

I thought happiness was vaguely connected with whimsical feelings when I talked to my friend, the disgraced judge, in 1973. I thought it came from having a good job, a loving family, and economic security. All those things are rewarding, of course. But I didn't know then that four years later my own life would be stripped of every single thing I thought essential for happiness.

Behind prison walls I discovered that happiness is an inside job. The happiest people I know are those who discover that real joy and fulfillment evolve as a byproduct of *creating* a meaningful life. And a *meaningful* life is created by making and then acting on eight fundamental choices. It doesn't matter who a person is, where he lives, or what his circumstances may be, anybody can create a meaningful life for himself by adopting these choices as his own.

1. Choose to live a God-centered life

It is no accident that the Bible begins with the elegantly simple declaration, "In the beginning God" (Genesis 1:1). A mature and personal relationship with God is essential for human happiness. But some people confuse fear with faith.

"All this God stuff is just a crutch for weak people," a prisoner once told me. I laughed, because he was recovering from knee surgery and leaned on two crutches as we talked. "Since crutches are for weak people, why don't you give me yours?" I asked.

"Are you crazy?" he growled. "I couldn't walk without 'em. I'd end up crippled for life!"

That's precisely the point. We're all badly wounded, bruised, and banged up by life. Every day we need faith in God's healing grace.

A God-centered life frees us to know who we are as persons: children of God, brothers and sisters to all others. A personal relationship with God liberates us from the anxiety of a meaningless existence. It drives us out of narrow, self-centered preoccupation with our own interests to minister to the needs of others.

God is the only secure foundation upon which we can create a meaningful life. No matter what we have to cope with, we know that "all things work together for good for those who love God and are willing to fit into His plans" (Romans 8:28, author's paraphrase).

2. Choose to be thankful

A friend of mine was going through some difficult times. A single mother with dependent children, she carried the parental and economic burdens alone.

"I don't have a magical solution to your problems," I admitted. "But I do have an idea. Write out a specific list of all your problems on one sheet of paper. On another sheet write an equally specific list of all the things for which you are thankful."

This is a process I've learned to use myself when I get to feeling like I'm walking all alone through a storm of trouble. It's always worked for me, but I wasn't sure she would really put her heart into the exercise.

"I'm on a natural high!" she laughed when I talked to her again a few days later. "I had eleven problems on my list. But then I ran out of paper when I tried to list all of my blessings. By then I was so happy and grateful, the problems didn't seem so large anymore."

Today, an important part of my friend's prayer life is spent in thanking God for all her blessings. Doing this regularly, even over a short period of time, has opened her life up to a deeper awareness of many little things she used to take for granted.

Focusing clearly on all the ways in which God is blessing us puts our problems in proper perspective.

We all have problems to deal with throughout our lives. But we're also surrounded with the lavishness of God's blessing. Our awareness of all the good things for which we can be thankful makes us happy and cheerful. My friend was so energized that she easily figured out a solution to several problems that had been blocked for months by worry.

3. Choose to be happy

"Rejoice, and be exceeding glad," Jesus told His disciples (Matthew 5:12, KJV). And Paul commanded Christian believers to "rejoice in the Lord always" (Philippians 4:4). Even in the most desperate suffering we can choose to be happy.

Viktor Frankl, a Jewish psychiatrist, experienced incomprehensible suffering in the Nazi death camps of World War II. Except for one sister, his entire family was wiped out during those savage times. Few men had better reason for hatred, bitterness, or cynicism.

But he chose a radically different response to brutality.

"We who lived in concentration camps can remember the men who walked through the huts comforting others, giving away their last piece of bread," he wrote. "They offer sufficient proof that everything can be taken away from a man but one thing—the last of the human freedoms: *To choose one's attitude in any given set of circumstances.*"

Happy people refuse to surrender the control of their freedom to choose happiness to any person or set of circumstances.

4. Choose to practice forgiveness

An unforgiven grudge and unresolved guilt are the two heaviest things in the universe. They crush the soul, smothering all joy and courage.

For years I carried a bitter grudge against a woman who willfully and maliciously did everything in her power to destroy my life. No matter how hard I tried to let the hostility go, it hung around me like thick fog over a swamp. So I wasn't cordial when she got through to me on the phone at the prison one day. "What do you want?" I snapped as soon as I recognized her voice.

"I just called to say I'm sorry if I've done anything to hurt you, and I'd like your forgiveness," she admitted nervously.

I almost choked on the bile in my throat. That *if* felt like another slap in the face. I wanted to tell her in the most colorful and graphic terms where to go with her request. But there's one big problem with telling people where to go: *They'll take you there with them!*

Jesus put the issue quite simply: "In the same way you judge others, you will be judged" (Matthew 7:2).

She hung up quickly when I told her she was forgiven. She never made any attempt to undo the damage she'd done to me, so I don't know what good it did *her*, but *I* suddenly felt wonderfully alive and free. Perhaps she didn't "deserve" forgiveness, but I deserved to be free from that crushing weight of hostility. Moreover, forgiveness is an act of grace, not a judicial balancing of the scales.

Life is difficult. Nobody lives long without becoming a victim of unfairness in some form: vicious gossip, broken relationships, or injury due to somebody else's negligence. Giving and receiving forgiveness is God's healing balm for our emotional and spiritual wounds. People who are quick to confess their own wrong and to forgive others for theirs are the happiest people, partly because they don't squander their lives carrying around a burdensome memory of past injuries received or inflicted.

5. Choose to love other people

To modify the lyrics of a popular song: People who love people are the happiest people in the world.

I know two sisters, now in their midforties, with similar histories. Both were sexually abused as children, and each endured twenty years of battering in marriages to alcoholic men. Both are intelligent, creative, gifted, and beautiful women. But here the similarity ends.

One is so badly wounded by her bitter history that she sours more with each passing year. Her face is heavily lined from years of scowling. She loathes all men. She's too abrasive and prickly for anyone to endure long as a friend. Nobody can get near her emotionally without being impaled on her sharp, hostile tongue.

Although no less wounded, her sister is remarkably different. She's a warm, cheerful, optimistic woman who loves other people openly and easily. She uses the pain in her own life like a radar—to make her incredibly sensitive to the feelings and needs of grieving people. I don't know of anybody who doesn't enjoy her company, especially when they're facing difficult times.

Admittedly, loving other people is risky business. We're never more vulnerable to injury than from people we love. And there's little protection against that possibility. But the second sister understands something about choices. "I know that loving people involves risk," she says. "But I choose to take that chance because there's one thing worse: Not taking the risk of giving and receiving love from other people."

Happy people know that love is like a kiss: We have to share it with somebody before we get anything of value from it.

6. Choose to retain a sense of humor

Humor is one of the soul's best weapons in the fight for self-preservation during difficult times.

A person going through the country stopped to talk with an old Maine farmer. "Are you working in the vineyard of the Lord?"

"No, them's soybeans," the farmer replied.

"Are you a Christian?"

"Nope. My name's Smith. There's a bunch of people by that name about three miles down the road."

"Are you lost?" asked the vexed visitor.

"Not on your life," the farmer replied easily. "Been living on this place all my life."

"Are you ready for the resurrection?"

"When is it?"

"Could be tomorrow or the next day or the next."

The farmer thought about this revelation for a moment before saying, "Well, don't tell my wife—she'll want to go all three days!"

Have you ever noticed how a good laugh can break the tension and brighten up your entire day? Laughter is indeed the best medicine!

Ed Ley, a Tennessee parole officer, works in a stressful job supervising ex-offenders released from prison. But he's a relaxed and cheerful man who takes everything in stride. His friends claim he's a walking encyclopedia of jokes and funny stories. It's hard to be glum around him.

Even Jesus used colorful humor, although it's easily missed because we've read the stories so often. "Don't pick at the speck of dust in your brother's eye when you have a plank sticking out of our own," He said (Matthew 7:3, author's paraphrase). Another time He told listeners, "It's easier for a camel to go through the eye of a needle than for a rich man to enter the kingdom of God!" (Matthew 19:24).

Can't you see the twinkle in His eye and the roar of laughter from those who heard Him use comical exaggeration to make a point?

Obviously, some things simply aren't funny: ethnic, racist, or sexist jokes, for example, or comedy that belittles marriage fidelity. But humor is a wonderful tool for relieving tension, anxiety, fear, and discouragement.

Happy people know when to be serious and when to chuckle. Remember, as Chesterton once cracked, "The angels fly so high because they take themselves lightly."

7. Choose to work at something meaningful

"One thing I know, the only ones among you who will be truly happy are those who will have sought and found how to serve others," Dr. Albert Schweitzer once told a group of young people. Although most people aren't called to a life of missionary service, the happiest people I know are those who *create* meaning in their work by finding ways to help others.

Bill, a resident of Hampton, Connecticut, is a retired salesman for vegetable seeds. Like many people, he was deeply touched as he became aware of the growing number of working poor and homeless people in America who were going hungry. But Bill wasn't content with just being touched by their plight; he decided to *do something* about it.

He took all his experience and knowledge about seeds and

planted a garden. Soon church members began helping him. In 1988 his small garden produced twenty-eight thousand pounds of food, which he contributed to the local food bank. Today, several other churches are planting gardens of their own and feeding thousands of hungry people.

Not everybody can plant a garden or go to Africa as a missionary. But *everybody* can do something to enrich the lives of others around them.

My wife, Edie, works as assistant to the director of personnel at the Tennessee Christian Medical Center in Nashville. With more than six hundred employees, the paperwork is always piling up because her routine work is interrupted so frequently with phone calls, complaints, questions, and sudden problems. But she's one of those rare people who really listens to others when they tell her of a problem.

"She was a lifesaver for me," one colleague admitted. "She even took time off from work one day to help me with a problem."

Her job is quite ordinary, but she chooses to make something meaningful out of her work by going the extra mile to help people, even when it doesn't fall under her technical job description. " 'Whatever you do, do it all for the glory of God,' " she says, quoting Paul to describe her philosophy on happiness (1 Corinthians 10:31). "Choosing to act on that command turns everything I do into a possibility for ministry."

The happiest people find ways to *make* their work meaningful in serving others.

8. Choose to be optimistic

"I am an optimist. It does not seem too much use being anything else," said Winston Churchill during the dark days of war. Regardless of their circumstances, happy people are optimistic and hopeful about life and the future.

Randall Dickman, thirty-four, is one of the happiest men I know. He's an incurable optimist—even though he's totally paralyzed from the neck down because of injuries sustained in an automobile wreck just three days before his eighteenth birthday. But that optimism didn't fall out of the sky; he *created* a meaningful life for himself, and that always leads to optimism.

How does a teenager cope with the realization that the rest

of his life will be spent in a wheelchair? How does he come to terms with the fact that acute, demoralizing pain will be a constant daily companion until the day of his death—which might come any day because of a lung infection? For months after his accident Randy struggled with alternating hope and despair—hope for recovery and growing despair as the list of things he would never do again got longer and longer.

He wanted to die. But he couldn't even kill himself without help. "I wish I were dead!" he told his mother one day.

Hope—only a glimmer at first—dawned in the form of an idea: "I can still use my mind!" Eventually, that hopeful thought drove him to make some hard choices, and then, acting on the choices available to him, thrust himself forward and out of his self-imposed wilderness of suicidal despair.

His first decision was to get a college degree and begin a career. It took him ten years of grueling work, but in 1984 he graduated *summa cum laude* with a B.S. degree in education. Today he's a happily married man, a father, and a popular high-school teacher in Savannah, Tennessee. Recently, he finished Tennessee's tough requirements to be a nursing home administrator.

Although each day brings him a long laundry list of special problems, he eagerly relishes the challenge of transforming obstacles into opportunities. "Years ago I realized that I had a fundamental choice to make," he says. "Either I could choose to focus on all my problems, or I could choose to spend my energy on possibilities. Since I didn't enjoy feeling miserable, I decided happiness is an option I'd take!"

One day he spoke to a group of convicts in my prison. He grinned as he looked over the audience. "When life hands you a lemon, an optimist is gonna find some way to create lemonade out of it," he laughed.

A man of deep spiritual faith, Randy Dickman chose to transcend his prison walls of pain and suffering by making and then *acting* on the eight choices available to him. He learned how to bloom where he was planted, no matter how rough and stormy life got for him.

One of the qualities that makes choosing happiness easier in difficult circumstances is tuning our ears to hear God speaking to us in both triumph and tragedy.

CHAPTER
Six

It's God Again

There's a scene in George Bernard Shaw's play, *St. Joan,* in which she's interrogated by French officers. "Where do you get your instructions?" they ask.

"I hear voices," Joan replies.

"How do you mean, voices?"

"I hear voices telling me what to do," she explains. "They come from God."

"Oh, your voices, your voices!" King Charles peevishly interrupts as he joins the interrogation. "Why don't the voices come to me? I am the king, not you."

"They do come to you, Sir, but you do not hear them," Joan of Arc says quietly.

Does that *Voice* still speak to us today?

The question may be an interesting abstraction to explore when life is serene and peaceful, but when our neat and orderly world crumbles before the chilling blast of real suffering, the question is profoundly personal and important. Then our souls ache to hear the word from God which Isaiah promised:

How gracious he will be when you cry for help!
As soon as he hears, he will answer. . . .
Whether you turn to the right or the left,
Your ears will hear a voice behind you, saying,
"This is the way; walk in it"
(Isaiah 30:19, 21).

For a person of faith, God's apparent silence hurts worse than anything else. During my thirteen years of wandering in the wilderness of prison, there have been long periods when God's voice was thunderously silent—or so it seemed. Those were the times I felt most terribly alone, abandoned, and cast off by Him. Yet in that very silence I have heard God's voice speaking most directly to me.

The Bible suggests four specific circumstances in which we may expect to hear God speaking to us. If we don't hear Him speaking to us today, the problem is in the receiver, not the transmitter.

1. God speaks to us in church and communal worship

For the most part we choose our messages when we choose our setting. Sports fans go to Yankee Stadium to see a baseball game, not to hear a Beethoven sonata. If you want to hear God's voice speaking to you, church is a good place to listen.

Zechariah was in church when an angel told him about the impending birth of John the Baptist. After many years of fasting and prayer, Simeon and Anna met Jesus in the temple shortly after His birth.

Jesus attended church regularly. "On the Sabbath day he went into the synagogue, as was his custom" (Luke 4:16). Even worshiping in small numbers brings a dramatic blessing. "Where two or three come together in my name, there am I with them," Jesus said (Matthew 18:20).

Sometimes it's easy to hear God speaking to us in church. We come to worship and things click. There's a sense of wonder: "Surely, the Lord is in this place. . . . This is none other than the house of God" (Genesis 28:16, 17). And, like Zechariah in the temple, we're moved and we do hear.

70

But it's not always easy. We come to worship out of habit, but we come feeling angry with somebody, or we're frustrated because painful circumstances have us in a maze and we can't find our way out. So we come to church as irritable critics. We've bought a ticket and expect a show. Someone is performing for us, and later we'll write up a review of it for delivery at dinner.

It's hard to hear God's voice above the roar of our own anger, fear, resentment, jealousy, or malice.

The fact is that in worship *we* are the performers and God is the audience. It may be that He writes up a review of how each of us did in worship! Did we hear His call to discipleship? Did we listen when we heard of a great need around us? Did we find our own way to give glory to God?

Admittedly, as Billy Graham says, kittens aren't biscuits just because they're born in an abandoned stove. And going to church, by itself, doesn't guarantee that we'll hear God's voice. But in opening our heart, mind, and soul during worship, Bible study, preaching, and prayer, we *will* hear God's voice calling us into personal discipleship.

2. God speaks to us in our work

With few exceptions, the Bible reveals that God first spoke to people when they were engaged in ordinary tasks. Moses was tending sheep. Saul was searching for lost cattle. Matthew was collecting taxes. Peter was fishing, and Paul was traveling to Damascus.

Unless God has broken the pattern completely, this means that God is most likely to speak to us while we are earnestly occupied at our business.

My friend Karen says God speaks to her almost every day. Before going off to work, she prays, asking God to use her to bring some cheer into the lives of the people she meets. She's a waitress. You might never notice her in a crowd, but she's one of God's saints because she sees her routine work as an opportunity to be a living witness to God's love.

"When I see hurting people, I know it's God again, calling me to answer," Karen says.

God rarely speaks to idle people. If we want to hear God's voice, we need to get busy and stay tuned!

3. God speaks to us through ordinary things

Perhaps because we're so saturated with the stunts and special effects of Hollywood, we'd like God to speak to us in a more dramatic voice. But the biblical pattern suggests something much more ordinary. When God speaks to people, it's usually through ordinary objects that take on special meaning. Moses saw a burning bush. Amos saw a plumb line. John the Baptist saw a dove. Paul saw a bright light.

My most intimate encounter with God's voice came on May 5, 1980, when I was transferred from jail to the state prison. My court appeals were exhausted, and so was I. It was the lowest point in my life. I badly needed to hear God's reassuring voice in the midst of a very personal nightmare.

It came in the form of a tiny, purple weed flower I discovered pushing its way through the packed earth on the prison yard. Something about that insignificant flower broke through my despair, and I heard God speaking to me through the color purple.

God whispers to us through ordinary things: the bread and wine of communion, the cross, art, music, and literature. He waits for us to hear. He waits for us to understand, and then share what He has said with the world. In the noisy tumult of life we need to tune out the chaos and listen if we want to hear "the still, small voice" of God speaking to us.

4. God speaks to us through our relationships

It is in our relationships with one another that God speaks to us most directly.

A parable is told about a poor cobbler whom God promised to visit in person. In preparation for this event, the cobbler fixed the best food, laid out fine clothes, and even made an exquisite pair of shoes for the Lord.

While waiting for the Lord, however, a starving man arrived, asking for food. The cobbler gave him something to eat. Later a widow with three children asked for food and clothing, and the cobbler helped her. As the day drew to a close, another beggar without shoes caught the cobbler's attention. Unable to bear the beggar's pain, the cobbler gave him the rest of his food and the shoes he'd made for the Lord.

"You promised to visit me today," the disappointed cobbler prayed at the end of the day. "Why didn't You come?"

Then God spoke to him. "But I did visit you. I came to you as the man in need of food, a mother and children in need of clothing, a barefoot man in need of shoes."

This story is similar to Jesus' parable of the sheep and the goats. And both suggest that the closest we will come on this earth to seeing God's face and hearing His intimately personal voice is when we *look* into the face of a person in need, *hear* his or her cry for help, and then *respond* to that need.

It's God again

God is burning bushes and dangling plumb lines all around us, if we will open our eyes to see them. The key sentence in the story of Moses is what he did when he saw the bush: " 'I will go over and see this strange sight' " (Exodus 3:3). How many times have you and I seen a "great sight," but then ignored it?

The real miracle is not in the bush or the plumb line but in the willingness of some people to see God's revelation in these ordinary things.

Elmer Sanderson, a retired Ford employee, saw a "plumb line" in young children, so he cultivated skills as a ventriloquist and created Buzzy Blue-eyes, a dummy that he uses to entertain children in church.

Pastor Conn Arnold sees a "burning bush" in the lives of prisoners who need his love and encouragement.

Julia "Grandma" Grow sees a "bright light" in the lives of retarded children. Today hundreds of these children have been blessed by God because of the love and care they found in the home she built to care for them.

God most frequently enters our lives through the back door. We need an alertness, an openness to receive Him. Do you know a person on whom all of life has fallen in, who is suffering through and through? That's God, coming to you for comfort. Do you know someone whose life has been soured by anger and bitterness? That's God again, coming to you for peace. Do you know someone whose life is closed in by prejudice, who cannot see God in His varied people? Even here, it's God again, and you hold the key to His imprisonment.

A child used to seeing the saints in beautiful stained glass said, "Saints are the people the light shines through." That's what people of faith are, and these are the people to whom God speaks.

One important way in which we hear God's voice speaking to us is in a call for forgiveness. The story in the next chapter is about a young woman who suffered near-death at the hands of the most depraved and evil man I've ever met. But it's more than a story of suffering; it's a story of a young woman's journey from hate to grace.

Although I've written some about the subject of forgiveness earlier in this book, I've included this story because I've seen just how deeply suffering can be exacerbated by the inability to forgive those who have offended us.

Seven

Forgiving the Unforgivable

Nancy Shelton, twenty-two, didn't expect her day to end in mind-numbing terror as she packed her yellow VW that Sunday morning, March 23.

"Please be careful," her father warned for the third time as he hugged her goodbye.

But she wasn't worried about anything as she left her home and headed south. She had seen enough human wreckage as a student nurse in the emergency room, so she knew that terrible things happen to people when they least expect it. But tragedy was something that happened to other people, something she heard about on the news. It had nothing to do with her life. Besides, she always prayed each day, asking God to protect her.

She believed deeply that He would.

Preoccupied with her own thoughts, she didn't notice the dark blue, late-model Ford pull in behind her as she exited the Beltway and merged with the southbound traffic on Interstate 95.

But John Dixon, thirty-four, an experienced human predator, noticed *her*. Convicted three times for vicious assaults on women, most of his adult life had been spent behind prison walls. In between prison sentences, however, he'd committed scores of other crimes against women for which he'd never been caught.

He smiled when he first spotted the attractive young woman and noticed that her car was packed with boxes and suitcases. Her tags were local, so his excitement grew as the miles passed. Clearly, she was traveling some distance.

"The chase for little foxes is on! Let the games begin!" he chortled, popping another pill in his mouth and gulping it down with tepid beer.

He loved *stalking* his potential victims. They weren't people to him, just exotic game to be tracked down and captured. He didn't mind chasing them for hundreds of miles, either. That was the part of the game he enjoyed most.

Unaware of her imminent peril and weary from the long drive, Nancy pulled off the interstate at twilight and parked in a rest stop. She felt safe because several other cars and a dozen eighteen-wheelers were parked nearby. After setting her watch alarm for forty-five minutes, she leaned back against a pillow to dose.

The nightmare begins

The sharp sound of knuckles rapping on her window startled her awake. Dazed and alarmed at the same time, she stared blankly at the friendly, smiling face peering in at her. She noted the scarring on his face from a bad case of adolescent acne.

"Sorry, I didn't mean to scare you," he said cheerfully. "But you've got a flat on the right rear tire."

She hesitated. Her doors were securely locked. The seconds ticked off.

"Well, do you want any help changing it?" he asked, glancing at his watch.

She looked him over carefully. He appeared quite ordinary. *I'm acting like a kid,* she thought, *scared of my own shadow. I should be grateful for help.* She sighed with relief and unlocked the door.

She froze when he jerked the door open and leaped at her, shoving her roughly back on the seat. "You make a sound, you're *dead!*" he hissed, jabbing a snub-nosed pistol into her throat. "You wanna die tonight?"

Too paralyzed to speak, she shook her head. The foul, sour smell of stale beer and cigarettes made her nauseous.

"We're gonna walk over to my car, and you're not gonna make a sound," he said calmly. "Do exactly what I say, or I'll blow your pretty head off," he warned, pulling her out of the car.

Her heart pounded so hard she vaguely wondered if it might explode as she looked into those pale, sinister eyes. She had no doubt he would murder her. "This can't be happening," she thought, looking around at all the other vehicles nearby. "God, why are You letting this happen to me? Somebody, please help me!"

She stumbled once, nearly falling, as they walked toward his car. But he caught her and jabbed the pistol into her ribs. "Don't even think about running," he growled. "Just do what you're told and you *might* live to see another day."

She climbed into his car on the driver's side and slid across the seat. He took a piece of cord from his jacket pocket and tied her hands and feet securely. She didn't have a coat on. It was cold. She couldn't stop shivering.

Hurriedly, he rifled her purse and found $823 in cash. "You don't mind if I keep this, do you?" he taunted amiably, shoving the cash into his shirt pocket.

"You can keep it, all of it, just let me go," she answered in a shaking voice. "I won't tell anybody."

He laughed at her.

For nearly an hour he drove around aimlessly, talking to her in an insanely friendly voice, while describing in the most vulgar and graphic terms what he was going to do to her. Once she started to cry. His fist shot out, hitting her squarely on the jaw.

"I don't wanna hear any of your blubbering!" he snarled.

Moments later she began waving her bound hands and screaming as a police car raced past them in the opposite direction. Dixon roared with laughter. He relished the terror he inflicted.

"Ain't nobody gonna help you tonight except me," he sneered.

Finally, he stopped at the end of a dirt road. After stripping her, he shoved and half-carried her into a wooded area where he knocked her down and tied her outstretched arms to two small trees. For several hours he abused and degraded her, laughing at her pleas for mercy, and viciously slapped her repeatedly in the face when she didn't respond as he demanded.

After spitting in her face, he stood up and looked down at her in contempt. Then he smashed the toe of his boot into her side. She felt the ribs give way.

"Now I've gotta decide what to do with you," he mused aloud. "Do I leave you here to die slowly of exposure, or just kill you and get it over with?"

She begged for her life again and again, until she realized he was having fun with her anguish. "Please, just get it over with," she whispered in utter despair.

He knelt over her body and seemed to be studying her. For the first time in her life, as she looked into his malignant, glittering eyes, she knew she was in the presence of something profoundly evil.

Her mind was a chaotic, jumbled collage of feelings. College, friends, all the good times. She could feel the warmth of her father's embrace, and she wondered how he would take the news of her death. She closed her eyes and waited for the end, thinking, *Oh, God, how could you let this happen to me?*

But Dixon slapped her and made her open her eyes. "I ain't never killed a woman before," he giggled happily, "and I've gotta make it last."

Our Father

She cowered under him as he slowly raised his clenched fist and then tried to jerk away as it crashed down on her face. But the ropes held her fast. Light exploded in her brain. The salty taste of blood flooded her mouth.

"Our Father, which art in heaven . . ." she whispered.

But his other fist shot out, and she felt the cartilage in her nose shatter. Two teeth broke loose.

"Hallowed be thy name. Thy kingdom come; thy will be done . . ."

He laughed hysterically as he pounded her face.

"Forgive us our sins as we forgive those . . ."

"No! Shut your ugly mouth and die!" he screamed.

"Lead us not into temptation . . ." she wept.

"I'll kill you if you don't shut up!" he bellowed. Through bloodied eyes she saw his face, twisted with hate and rage. He grabbed a large rock in both hands and raised it over her head, aching to crush the life out of her in one final blow.

"Deliver us from evil . . ." she whispered.

Suddenly, Dixon's fingers went numb. From out of the darkness he saw a faint, glowing light. It grew larger, coming closer, and he could see the state's electric chair advancing toward him. His name was engraved in bright, colorful lights on the back of the chair that kept blinking on and off.

The rock dropped from his shaking hands, missing her head by inches. He scrambled to his feet, backing away, waving his arms in front of him as though warding off some invisible enemy. The demonic rage in his face vanished, replaced by pure terror.

Barely conscious, Nancy heard the car door slam and the motor start. Pieces of earth and broken leaves rained down on her battered body from the spinning wheels as he fled, leaving her alone in the darkness.

It took more than an hour for her to work free from the ropes. Almost blind and in shock from the beating and exposure, she staggered through the woods for a long time until she became dimly aware of distant lights, and the sound of cars caught her attention.

The Harrisons, an elderly couple who ran a convenience store just off the interstate, gasped when the naked and badly beaten woman stumbled into the store and collapsed at their feet.

"God, please help me," she mumbled as she lost consciousness.

Don't kill me

Dixon used some of the money he stole from her purse to check into a rundown motel less than ten miles from where he'd left his victim. He was sure she would die soon and her body wouldn't be discovered for months, if ever. He turned on the TV, trying to drown out the sound of her echoing screams, and settled down for some heavy drinking. His hands shook badly as he popped one pill after another into his mouth, hoping the chemicals would erase the memory of what he'd seen.

An hour later he sank into a drunken stupor.

But detectives got a good description of him and his car when Nancy briefly regained consciousness in the hospital. Police radios bristled with details of the brutal attack and a warning that Dixon was armed and considered dangerous.

Two off-duty officers spotted his car during the early morning hours and called for a backup. Within minutes a large force of heavily armed, tight-lipped lawmen surrounded the motel. When they burst into the room, they found Dixon cowering in the bathroom.

"Don't kill me! Please, don't kill me!" he screamed as a dozen shotguns pinned him to the floor.

He waived his rights to remain silent forty-five minutes after detectives completed their "preliminary interview"— which consisted of a beating administered by furious police officers. He confessed to the attack on Nancy, and then for six hours gave investigators a bone-chilling account of his life as a serial rapist.

They thought his confession gave them an airtight case. But a week later his court-appointed attorney challenged the legality of his confession. "The man was drunk when you people interrogated him at the end of a blackjack," he argued. "He was in no condition to intelligently waive his right to counsel."

Privately, the exasperated county prosecutor knew he was right. "You guys got overeager and botched it," he snapped at the frustrated detectives. "Now one of you hotshots has to tell the victim she'll have to come back and testify at his trial because he's going to plead not guilty!"

Trial by ordeal

Detective-sergeant Phil Conrad, sixty-three, a hard-nosed, savvy street cop and a deeply committed Christian, volunteered for the assignment. Ordinarily, a policewoman would have handled most contact with a rape victim. But a special bond had evolved between the aging cop and Nancy when he stood by and held her hand for two hours that night in the emergency room. His face was the first thing she saw when she regained consciousness. Her own terror softened when she saw a silent tear run down his weather-beaten cheek.

He found her standing in front of a mirror in her hospital room, staring bitterly at her disfigured and swollen face. "Look at what that animal did to me! And now he says he didn't do it!" she shouted through cracked lips.

Gently, Conrad turned the young woman around and examined her face closely. "I've seen a lot of beaten faces like yours," he admitted. "But the doctors have done a good job on you. Six months from now you'll be like new again."

"No, I won't," she muttered angrily. "I'll *never* be the same again.

"Yes, you will," he insisted. "But the hidden wounds will take longer. That takes another kind of surgery." She heard what he said, but she didn't respond.

Within three months Nancy had recovered sufficiently from her injuries to work. But the sparkle had disappeared from her eyes. Life had turned sour. During the day bitterness and hatred for Dixon chewed away at her consciousness like a determined rat after a piece of cheese. She murdered him in her mind a thousand times, subjecting him to the most Draconian horror her imagination could conjure up before crushing the life out of him.

But he wouldn't stay dead.

Nights were the worst. She relived the ordeal in a long series of nightmares. She always woke up, shaking and screaming, just as the rock came down on her head. What his fist had failed to accomplish, her memory of him finished off.

Such penetrating, abiding hatred was a foreign experience to her. And so was the bitter resentment and hostility she felt toward God for not helping her. By the time she testified at Dixon's trial ten months later, the five-foot six-inch woman barely tipped the scales at ninety-two pounds.

The defendant stared at her impassively, bored and disinterested as she described in a choking voice the nature of her injuries: three broken ribs, a broken nose and fractured jaw, the loss of two front teeth, numerous lacerations and contusions, and blurred vision in one eye. Specialists didn't know if her vision would ever return to normal.

At the last minute Dixon refused to take the stand. The judge was visibly unhappy with his decision to rule the confession inadmissible, but the law was clear. The jury would hear nothing of Dixon's admissions or his prior record.

The jury was composed of seven men and five women. They were quick in their verdict of guilt. But they struggled to agree on a sentence. Some demanded life. Others insisted on something less. Finally, a compromise of thirty years was accepted. They didn't know Dixon would be eligible for parole in ten years.

The defendant turned and winked at Nancy when the verdict was read.

Asking the right questions

"I feel like I've been raped again," Nancy complained bitterly as she sat with Sgt. Conrad in his car, waiting for her flight at the airport. The relatively light sentence seemed to mock her suffering, belittling and trivializing what she'd gone through.

"There's nothing we can do about his sentence," Conrad said. "You can be sure the jury didn't understand how the parole system works. But you've got to put this thing behind you."

Nancy wasn't listening. "I just don't understand why God allowed this to happen to me!" she cried out in frustration. "*Why?*"

"I don't know," Conrad admitted. "But maybe you're not asking the right question. I try to teach rookie detectives that asking the wrong question will lead in circles, to false conclusions, or irrelevant answers."

"What does that have to do with me?"

He hesitated. "Maybe you would feel better if you thanked God for saving your life, instead of asking questions to which there are no answers."

Her face tightened in anger. "Oh, I get it. I not only have to live with what he did to me, but I'm supposed to feel guilty about how I feel too!" Her voice dripped with heavy sarcasm and self-pity.

Conrad studied her silently for several minutes before

speaking again. "Tell me something," he said softly. "What makes you the exception to the rule that the rest of us have to live with all the unfairness and uncertainty of life?"

She looked at him in shocked disbelief. "How can you be so cruel?" she whispered.

"It sounds cruel because you're not really hearing me," he replied. "I'm trying to get you to understand something: Even as you and I speak, millions of people are starving to death around the world. Most of them are children. Political prisoners are being tortured in a dozen countries. Before this day is out, hundreds of innocent victims will be robbed, raped, beaten, or killed by criminals across the country." He sighed heavily. "Life isn't as neat or orderly as you thought. Terrible, incomprehensible things happen to good people all the time, and there's rarely a 'good' answer to any of it."

He waited for her to speak, but she stared silently out the window.

"There is no rational explanation for evil," he continued. "It wouldn't be evil if you could explain or justify it. There is no meaning in evil by itself; it exists only to hurt people and God."

In spite of her anger, she looked at him curiously. "How does what happened to me hurt God?"

He shrugged. "Think about it. Jesus called Satan a liar and the father of all murderers. He hates God, but the only way he can get at God is through people. If you really want to cause parents the deepest suffering, hurt one of their children. Worse yet, make the child think the parents are either responsible or indifferent to his suffering."

He patted the young woman's shoulder awkwardly. "Job asked God the same questions you've asked. But God didn't give him an intellectual answer. He gave him something better—Himself."

This line of thought was a new idea for Nancy. Somehow, it made God seem closer, more involved with her life. She squeezed the cop's rough hands. "Anybody ever tell you that you'd have made a terrific theologian?" she asked.

He grinned. "All good detectives are frustrated theologians. But now the big question: Do you really want to be free of Dixon and his haunting memory?"

"Yes, I'd give anything to stop thinking about him. But how?"

"Forgive him," Conrad said bluntly.

"*Forgive* that monster for what he did to me!" she shouted. "Why? He doesn't deserve forgiveness! Surely, God can't demand that of me!"

"You're absolutely right," the detective agreed. "But *you* deserve to be free of the bitterness and hostility that's been eating you alive all these months. God makes that kind of healing possible through the sacrament of forgiveness."

She shook her head defiantly. "How can you forgive somebody who won't even admit he's done wrong?"

Two methods of forgiveness

Conrad chewed on his lower lip, considering his words carefully. "Keep in mind that I'm just an old cop ready for retirement, not a theologian. But I think there are two methods of forgiveness. One is more fulfilling than the other, but both lead to spiritual and emotional healing of the hidden wounds.

"First, there is the *forgiveness of reconciliation*," he continued as he turned in his seat to face her. "Somebody hurts you but later apologizes and asks for your forgiveness. When you offer the gift of grace in forgiveness, estrangement is turned into reconciliation. Trust is restored. The gaping spiritual wound between you is healed."

Nancy interrupted him. "You're asking me to let him off the hook, to not hold him accountable for his acts," she argued.

Conrad shook his head emphatically. "I'm not concerned about him at the moment. I'm trying to show *you* how to let *yourself* off the 'hook' of all those hurtful feelings. Now listen a minute.

"Second, there is the *forgiveness of judgment*. That's where meaningful reconciliation isn't possible, usually because the offender either doesn't want it or doesn't ask for it. But *you* don't do the judging. You forgive by giving up your right to judge the offender. By faith you turn it all over to God to sort out.

"This is what Jesus did when He asked God to forgive those who were nailing Him to a cross," he continued. "In order to protect *Himself* from normal human feelings of rage, hatred, and bitterness toward those who were snuffing out His life, He gave them and their judgment entirely over to God. Jesus knew that harboring those corrosive feelings would cut off the flow of God's grace in His life."

An hour later Nancy settled into her seat and fastened the belt across her lap. She could see Sgt. Conrad waving at her from across the tarmac. His parting words echoed in her mind: "Remember, you can't change what has happened to you. The only freedom you have left now is in choosing how you will respond to what has happened to you."

Silently, she prayed, thanking God for her life and the grandfatherly cop. "Lord, I turn John Dixon over to You in forgiveness. Heal him of his evil, even as You are freeing me now."

She could feel her own spirit soaring as the airplane climbed into the late afternoon sky, and God's warm grace flowed back into her life.

Epilogue

The names and other identifying data in this story were changed to protect Nancy's privacy. Fifteen years have passed since Dixon was tried and sentenced to prison. Since then Nancy has married and is the mother of two boys. "Thanks to Sgt. Conrad and God's grace, my life has never been better," she says.

Dixon, who claimed to be a born-again Christian, was paroled after serving twelve years. Six months later he was arrested again. While on parole he averaged one attack a week on a score of women. He's now serving a life sentence in another state. He won't be eligible for parole until he's eighty-three years of age.

What do you say to somebody when they're suffering some terrible loss? How do you bring comfort and mediate God's grace in ways that are meaningful to them? The next chapter looks at the other side of the coin of suffering: What do you do when your friend suffers?

CHAPTER
Eight

When Your Friend Suffers

I once had a client, a county politician, who was arrested and charged with sexually propositioning a policeman. Although a happily married man and the father of four children, Jim Bender (a pseudonym) also was somewhat effeminate. A cultural stereotype exacerbated his victimization. His protests of innocence fell on deaf ears.

The news media had a field day with such a salacious scandal. Jim's wife was humiliated with questions whenever she appeared in public. His children were tormented at school. Convinced of his guilt by what appeared to be overwhelming evidence—a policeman's charges—friends were uncomfortable around him and withdrew their support.

He wandered around in a daze for weeks, well aware that his political career was finished no matter how the trial ended.

In fact, the evidence against Jim was at best *under*-whelming! In court we proved conclusively that the arresting officer had a long history of homosexual activity. When confronted with the evidence during cross-examination, the officer claimed fifth-amendment rights against self-incrimination and refused to testify further.

An angry jury found Jim *not* guilty in record time.

Outside the courtroom an old friend timidly approached Jim. "I know I let you down," he apologized. "I felt so bad for you. I wanted to do something to help change things for you, but I didn't know how. I felt so frustrated."

It took some effort for Jim to be gracious, but he let his friend down easily. Later, however, he stated his feelings quite bluntly: "I needed the warmth of his friendship during the worst period of my life, not some magical solution. But he wanted to play God instead. No wonder he was frustrated!"

Human existence is riddled with the dark stain of suffering. Life can be brutally unfair at times. But knowing that to be true doesn't make the experience any less devastating for us when we are victimized. When we've been badly hurt, we need reassurance from our friends that we're loved, wanted, needed, and appreciated. Only caring family and friends can restore our sense of value when we feel most valueless.

But there is little in life that leaves us feeling more inadequate or incompetent than when we're faced with the bleak reality of a person we care about who is caught in the throes of suffering. What can we do? What can we say that will make a difference? What if we say or do the wrong thing?

A friend of mine put it quite simply: "I want to help when a friend is hurting, but I freeze up because I don't know how. So I withdraw, and then I feel guilty because I've let them down."

If we're honest about it, most of us have experienced the same thing at one time or another in our lives. And the truth is that there's little we can do or say to fix another person's problem or change the circumstances that have caused their suffering. But there are specific things we can do in a structured way that will help our friend to survive the pain, process it more efficiently, and then find his or her own path beyond prison walls of anguish.

1. Trust God to lead you

Before trying to help somebody else, we first have to come to terms with our own human limitations. We're not God, so we are not omnipotent. We're painfully human, limited in wisdom and resources. Unlike Jesus, we can't bring the dead back to life, heal people of disease, or restore their broken relationships.

But we *always* can do something meaningful to help.

I pray before reaching out to touch someone in pain. I ask God for two things: That He will comfort and bless my hurting friend, and that He will give me the wisdom, sensitivity, and creativity to be the answer to my own prayer.

I believe God takes such prayers very seriously. "Let go and let God" sounds good, but too many people use that idea as a pious cloak to hide behind—a self-serving justification for safe passivity.

Pastor Waumbrand tells a story about a church in Romania that decided to have a day of prayer for the hungry. Everybody in the community gathered at the cathedral on the appointed day. Some even gloated about their own piety when they noticed that a wealthy farmer in the village wasn't present. Toward the end of the service, however, the farmer's son appeared, carrying two huge sacks of grain on his shoulders.

He walked to the front of the church and dropped the sacks in front of the altar. Then he turned and looked at his neighbors. "My father has *sent* his prayer," he said.

Extraordinary people are ordinary people who pray for God's guidance and then pay attention on a consistent basis to the little things in life that God brings to their attention. They don't squander their time or energy on grand but empty gestures. They focus on what they can do, and then they just do it.

God relishes a chance to work in partnership with those who love Him and are willing to serve as a human vehicle for His healing grace. But only those who trust God to lead them are free enough to accept their limitations and still give the most precious gift of all to a suffering friend—love.

2. Affirm their value by loving them

Dick Snyder, an accountant at the Tennessee Christian Medical Center, is one of the smartest men I know when it comes to using ordinary skills to comfort people. While walking down a hospital corridor recently, he glanced into an office and saw a mutual friend of ours slumped at her desk.

"Problems?" he asked. She nodded without speaking. "Do

you need to talk?" She shook her head. He hesitated. "Do you need a hug?" She nodded silently, stood up, and let him hug her while she fought back the tears.

Although his gesture might have been misunderstood by some, it was a profoundly human act. He preferred to risk being misunderstood than risk leaving her hurting. He didn't solve her problem, but his caring warmth energized her sufficiently to deal with it herself.

Pastor Conn Arnold, a popular volunteer prison chaplain, is highly regarded behind the walls of the Tennessee State Penitentiary. It takes him half an hour to move thirty yards through the compound because he stops to hug, backslap, and shake hands with the roughest convicts behind the walls. "Man, it's good to see you again," he tells one man. To another: "I really appreciate you."

"He just makes you feel good about yourself, no matter what might be wrong, because you know he cares," a prisoner says.

He isn't afraid to openly love people, even convicts. Although he moved to Washington, D.C., five years ago, rarely does a day go by when some inmate doesn't ask me, "Where's Conn these days? When is he gonna be here to visit again?"

When God wants to hug us, He always sends somebody to put His arms around us. That's one way in which people mediate God's grace most dramatically to one another, especially during rough times. But a lot of pain goes unhealed because the people God sends don't go!

Never assume that your friend knows you love and care for him. During difficult times, silence or vague generalities are almost always experienced as indifference. Be direct and specific. Nothing pulls the broken pieces of a shattered life back together faster than the certain knowledge that we're loved by other people.

3. Let them ventilate

While in college I worked part time at a hospital. One day I accidentally jostled a patient's bed while trying to make him comfortable. "Are you trying to kill me?" he shouted. "Leave me alone!"

I didn't understand the outburst, but an experienced nurse

saw what had happened. "Don't take it personally," she advised. "Hurting people are touchy people."

Whether wounded in body or spirit, hurting people are indeed touchy at times. They're quite capable of lashing out angrily and unreasonably at those closest to them. Faith in God is stretched to the breaking point. Marriages and other close relationships may crack under the stress of suffering, often because of what somebody said or didn't say at the right moment.

A warm and caring pastor came to visit me when I was going through the early days of adjusting to prison life. He wanted to assure me that God loved me and was working for good in my life, regardless of how things looked at the moment.

"If this is an example of God helping me, I don't think I'll survive much more of it!" I snapped harshly. He studied me thoughtfully and listened while I vented a lot of bitterness and self-pity.

"I know what you mean," he sighed when I finally ran out of steam. "I've had times in my own life when I thought I hated God. Fortunately, as things worked out, I'm glad I got over it. I finally realized that honest anger at God is an acknowledgement of His power and love."

His candid admission caught me by surprise. I realized that he not only listened—really hearing my words; he heard beyond them to where I was struggling with issues of faith. He clearly understood the grieving process, so I could trust him and listen to him when I had nothing more to say.

Hurting people need to talk it out with a friend they can trust to really hear them. That's one of the important ways in which we sort through the broken rubble when the storm has passed and we begin putting the muddled pieces back together. We need to talk with someone who will listen without censoring or lecturing us for our outbursts of anger, bitterness, or resentment.

Grief is the human response to suffering, and that process follows a fairly predictable spiritual and emotional sequence.

First comes shock—a paralyzing experience of bewildered numbness. Shock is followed by denial: "This *can't* be happening to me!" What follows is chaotic, exhausting, and emotionally explosive: anger, bitterness, resentment, and self-pity. People are quite capable of saying the most outrageous things when trapped by such destructive feelings. Let them ventilate. It's part of the process. As Job discovered, there is no shortcut to reaching acceptance at the end of grieving.

Angry and bitter feelings are usually disguised by classic Why questions: Why is this happening? Why has God allowed this? What have I done to deserve this? Why is God punishing me so harshly?

These are trap questions because rarely is there a clear answer—at least not readily obvious at once. Trying to answer these questions only leads to "Why not," "Yes but" confusion because the questions are rooted in anguish and brokenness, a cry of pain, not a serious invitation to abstract theological discussion.

Job's "comforters" clearly did not understand that!

People don't need—nor are they likely to hear—a lecture on the meaning of suffering when their heart is breaking from grief. Even God didn't answer any of Job's questions until Job got some of the anger out of his system. Ultimately, God gave Job *Himself,* not answers to impossible riddles.

Don't try to answer Why questions when your friend is grieving. Give him your God-centered, loving self. Listen to him. Accept your limitations and do what you can. Then God can filter His gracious love through you and begin the process of healing.

4. Grieve with them

A friend of mine is a very successful and popular pastor, but that hasn't always been true. "I used to be so heavenly minded I wasn't any earthly good," he says dryly.

He's always loved people deeply, but he was raised in a time when men didn't show their feelings. It was somehow unmanly, a weakness. Worse, at the seminary he was warned to "keep some emotional distance" between himself and his parishioners. So he learned to distrust his own feelings, to fear others, and to distance himself from both.

"I preached technically perfect sermons, but nobody was touched," he admits. "I baptized, counseled, married and buried people. But my life got emptier with each passing year."

One day as he preached a funeral for a young boy, he looked out over the congregation. The grieving mother caught his eye and held it, and his mind went blank. She looked at him hopefully. What did she want? What did she need from him? At that moment the tragic death of a small boy collided with the meaninglessness of his own life and ministry. He broke down and wept before his astonished people.

"I thought I'd failed my parishioners by losing control like that, and I started to apologize to the mother," he told me. "But she stopped me and hugged me. She said, 'Thank you for grieving with me over my baby.'"

It hasn't been easy, but my friend has slowly learned the value of opening up his heart to the feelings of other people. And in the process he has become a more effective pastor. His people are blessed, and his life is richer and more meaningful.

There are mysteries in suffering we cannot understand, but I'll give you one that we can: The weight of a heartbreak shared with a loving friend is cut in half. When the burden is shared with many people, we can cope with almost anything. We never feel more revitalized than when a friend loves us enough to grieve with us in our pain.

5. Expect the best from your friend

For the past thirteen years I have been serving a ninety-nine-year prison term in one of America's most wretched prisons. I live in a demented world where some of the most violent, hate-filled men are packed together like sardines in a can. I'd be rich if I had a dollar for every time my life has been directly or indirectly threatened. Drugs, murder, robbery, sexual perversion, corruption, and every other form of vice known to humankind flows through here like raw sewage under city streets.

I didn't think I would survive the first year with either my mind or spirit intact. I've struggled through long periods when I wondered if God was making me into a modern-day Job II. Everything that could go wrong in my life, *did*.

Dealing with the savage men surrounding me was bad enough, but I also had to deal with some equally savage staff members. Although most prison employees are hard-working, dedicated people who are overworked and underpaid, a significant minority are even more vicious than the prisoners they control. They look for opportunities to abuse and degrade the inmates, while wheeling and dealing with others in smuggling drugs, weapons, and alcohol into the prison. The only difference between these people and prisoners is the uniform they wear.

But today I'm profoundly happy, contented—and still in prison. Yet my trust in God, love for people, and general optimism about life have grown stronger with each passing year.

Why?

It's simple. In addition to what I've already written in this book, my life has been blessed with scores of loving friends, in addition to my family. Every month brings many letters, cards, tapes, and notes to my cell from children and adults of all ages. They communicate incredible warmth and affection. Although I'm not quite sure why, they appear to love, admire, and respect me. They expect the very best from me at all times—not as a demand but as a manifestation of their confidence in me.

It's a challenge that's impossible to resist.

When Jesus entered the Garden of Gethsemane on that last night before His suffering on the cross, He desperately needed His friends. " 'My soul is overwhelmed with sorrow to the point of death. Stay here and watch with me,' " He said to Peter, James, and John (Matthew 28:38).

He didn't expect them to *fix* His problems. He knew they couldn't. What He needed was something they could give: their prayers, loving support, and listening ears, their empathy and their confidence. That would not have changed His circumstances, but He would have found comfort in those circumstances.

Instead they slept.

It's important to have faith in God and other people. But it's equally important to know that both have faith in us, especially when we're going through hard times. When we know for sure that we are loved, by both God and other people, any form of adversity is relatively easy to transcend, at least in time.

But don't try to foist some contrived "confidence" on your friend unless you have prayed for guidance, done all you can in spite of your limitations, loved him to the best of your ability, allowed him to ventilate his honest feelings, and grieved with him. Otherwise, you will not be taken seriously.

I've never met a person who didn't have problems. But many people lack a structured way in which to approach problem solving with solid biblical principles. In the story of David and Goliath I discovered a series of five principles that show how every problem can be managed effectively.

Nine

How Do You Solve a Problem?

I called my wife at home one night to find her over-whelmed with a variety of problems that had suddenly burst over the calm of her life. "I feel like I'm sur-rounded by an army of giants," she said tiredly. "They've knocked me flat, and they're doing the Mexican hat dance on my prone body!"

You've probably had days like this yourself.

As you read this chapter in the security of your home or office, you may feel safe at the moment. But soon you'll have to get up and face the giants. Some of these giants are huge, ugly creatures with mean dispositions. Others are medium-sized giants with whom you're intimately acquainted because they've been around for so long. A few are small. They're like a nagging irritant. But there are so many of them. Like cockroaches, no matter what you do, they keep coming back.

Every day of our lives, in one form or another, we're chal-lenged by the giants—those frustrating, intractable problems, temptations, and conflicts that march destructively through the middle of our lives. They stand between us and a mean-ingful Christian life. We're inheritors of a gospel that prom-ises "abundant life" here and "eternal life" to come. But again and again we're robbed of the fulfillment of that promise. It's carried away like plunder by the giants we can't seem to defeat.

How do we defeat a giant?

David confronted this problem three thousand years ago in a dramatic, deadly encounter with Goliath, an enormous giant (see 1 Samuel 17:1-58). He stood nine feet tall and was as strong as a bull—without benefit of anabolic steroids! The tip of his spear alone weighed fifteen pounds.

For forty days he waved that spear lightly in his massive hand, taunting the soldiers of Israel. "Are you men of Israel cowards?" he roared. "Send someone out to fight me!" Whether or not the Israelites were cowards is debatable. But they cer-tainly weren't stupid—no one came out to fight!

David arrived at the worst of the crisis, bringing food from his father for his older brothers, and he couldn't believe what he saw and heard. There was Goliath, hurling ridicule and insults at Israel, and they took it in terrified silence. And do you know what David found the Israelites doing about this problem giant? They were having our equivalent to an official church board meeting! The Goliath problem was being dis-cussed at length. They probably even had flip charts and plans and graphs and budgets and projects and a great debate about who was responsible for the man.

David finally defeated Goliath himself with a slingshot and a few small stones. There's no mystery about how this in-triguing Bible story ends. But in terms of confronting the problem giants in our own lives, what is of value in this story are the *five principles* David followed in resolving the problem of Goliath once and for all. Consider the problems you face, and see if David's strategy doesn't work just as well for you.

1. It is God's fight

Have you ever wondered how David mustered up the courage to tackle nine-foot Goliath with just a slingshot? Was he blessed with a larger dose of courage than most? Or was he so macho about having killed a lion and a bear that he was foolishly oblivious to the real danger posed by tangling with this enormous Philistine?

David answered that question when he met Goliath in combat: "I come against you in the name of the Lord Almighty. . . . For the battle is the Lord's," he shouted (1 Samuel 17:45, 47).

You don't have to fear any giant when you know the battle is the Lord's. But the real problem for most of us when we're surrounded by giant problems is a hard question: Is the Lord *really* with me?

Prison is a dreadful place to be, especially for those young men who are small in physical stature. They're easily victimized by the predatory bullies who roam every prison like a pack of wild dogs in search of fresh prey. I've seen scores of these youngsters backed into a corner until their only way out was to get a knife and kill the bully tormenting them. Most don't resort to such a drastic remedy; they simply surrender, and every day of their lives behind prison walls is pure hell on earth.

Knowing this, I was surprised when I met two young brothers who fearlessly walked the prison yard. In spite of their small size, nobody bothered them. In fact, the typical convict shark treated them with measured respect. Another prisoner laughed when I asked what accounted for their obvious immunity. "Have you ever seen their father?" he chuckled.

He then told me about the boys' father, a tough mountain man from east Tennessee, who intentionally got himself arrested and sent to prison so he could look after his sons. He didn't baby them. He expected them to conduct themselves like men. But he also let it be known that anybody unwise enough to attack his sons would have to deal with him—"up close and personal!" he warned.

After three years he was paroled and left his sons behind. But they were safe. Nobody doubted for a minute that he would come back—in a hurry—if his sons needed him.

This remarkable, self-sacrificing father reminds me of God. We're all prisoners, trapped in a world of powerful, dangerous giants. But in the incarnation of Jesus Christ, God joined us in our prison to help us fight and defeat the destructive giants in our lives.

David wasn't macho or foolish. He simply knew his Father. Years later he would compose the twenty-third psalm that has brought such great comfort to millions of people as they faced big problems: "Yea, though I walk through the valley of the shadow of death, I will fear no evil: for *thou art with me*" (Psalm 23:4, KJV, emphasis supplied).

Every month I receive many letters from people who have read my books and articles. Invariably, they ask me the same question: "How do you endure such circumstances and keep your sanity intact?" My answer is always the same: *faith.* Without the awareness that God is with us, even small problem giants can trip us up. With faith in God as a shield, even the toughest problem giants can be defeated.

2. Attack the giant at hand

The Philistines were not Israel's only enemy. There were the Ammonites, the Phoenicians, and the Midianites. David could have volunteered for service on some distant front. Who could have blamed him if he had? After all, he was a mere boy going up against a giant who would have made Larry Bird of the Boston Celtics look like he suffered from growth retardation.

But Goliath was the giant causing the problem, so David attacked him first.

Most of us have a large herd of giants waiting in ambush for us at home, at our work, at school, or in church. So at the beginning of a hard day, make your giants line up and count off. It's the simplest and most effective rule for giant killing and the best advice I ever got for getting things done.

When I forget this principle, my day quickly deteriorates into a blur of frenzied activity as I rush off in every direction. I end up throwing a harmless wad of paper at one giant, shouting pointlessly at another, and making faces at a third. At the end of the day I'm worn out, and there they are, still laughing at me. In the morning I know they'll be waiting for me again, bigger and meaner than ever because I let them grow some more.

What is your biggest problem? What is it that so clouds your day with anxiety and discouragement, robbing you of all the joy God intends? Is your marriage in a mess? Have your children become hostile strangers? Are you drinking too much? Is your career floundering? Do you feel alienated and estranged from God and everybody else?

These are heavy, mean-spirited giants, and most of us wear ourselves out because we carry them around piggyback all day instead of attacking them directly.

There's an old English benediction that says, "From ghoulies and ghosties and long-leggety beasties and things that go bump in the night, Good Lord, deliver us!" But if we're honest about it, we know that what usually goes bump in the night for us is the giant that sat around our office or living room all day, leering and laughing and hurling insults at us because we were afraid to tackle it.

So line those giants up. Make a list of Giant #1, Giant #2, and Giant #3. Start at the top. Deal with the giant at hand, get him buried, and then get on to the next one. But don't try to fight the whole team at once. Giant killing is not a team sport! Don't try to tackle them all at once unless you want to get buried yourself.

"Sufficient unto the day is the evil thereof," Jesus said (Matthew 6:34, KJV). Take the giants on one at a time, and don't worry about it if you don't get the whole team finished off in a week, a month, or even a year. Take on the giant at hand. Every day is a new start, and by God's grace some of those giants will be dead and gone.

3. Use the weapons you have

David faced the same problem you and I have: He had to destroy the giant before Goliath destroyed him. But how was he to do it? Some warned him it was a hopeless task in the first place. Others laughed at him for thinking he, of all people, could do it. Saul tried to help by giving the boy his own armor. David tried it on, but he looked as silly as he felt in the oversized suit.

David settled for what he had available.

I know a single mother with five teenage children who faced some enormous giants. Divorce and financial pressure had shattered the family dreams. The mother barely made enough to keep a roof over their heads. Without help from the children's father—which wasn't forthcoming—she couldn't help them achieve their goal of attending a Christian college.

It looked as though she and her children were doomed to become another entry in the poverty statistics about single mothers with dependent children. Demoralized and discouraged, the entire family began unraveling with complaints, faultfinding, and recriminations.

But then a friend showed them how they could pool their money (the children had part-time jobs), cut expenses to the bone, and begin to get ahead without help from anybody else. Each one could do little or nothing alone, but together their combined resources were sufficient. Today, the two oldest children are at a Christian college. The third will follow soon, and the two youngest are chomping at the bit to get started.

They discovered that their greatest resource was within themselves: their commitment to one another as a family and their faith in God. With that, plus some imagination, creativity, and hard work, they found that *all* their goals were attainable. Today, the entire family is achieving great success because they quit complaining about what they didn't have and began using the resources they had—no matter how limited.

Perhaps Jesus wished at times that He had some heroic characters or distinguished theologians to recruit as His disciples. But He didn't have any. So He began with what He had available: a radical politician, a tax collector, several fishermen, and assorted Galileans who were more available than able. But look at what Jesus was able to accomplish with this unlikely collection of people!

Begin with what you have. Wishing you had a new wife or husband, better behaved teenagers, a thoughtful boss, or more sensitive parents won't make it so. You won't suddenly have a perfect family, church, workplace, personal discipline, or prayer life. But you can start today with what you've got right now.

Rossini, the famous Italian composer, was asked to write a special opera for a group whose contralto had only one good note—a middle B-flat. He must have liked the challenge of such an absurd proposition because he went to work and created an aria for the contralto, weaving a lovely harmony around it for the orchestra and chorus.

That's what God does for you and me when we use the

weapons we have at hand to fight the giants in our lives. At times we may feel like we've only got one good note to play on our best day. But God can take that one note, if we're open and willing to be led, and create a brilliant masterpiece out of our lives with it.

David started with the weapons he had available. If you and I are ever to be successful in defeating the giants wreaking havoc in our lives, we must do the same.

4. Keep it simple

The architects and engineers of the El Cortez Hotel in San Diego thought they had an enormous problem a few years ago when they tried to decide where to install the elevator. A janitor overheard their conversation. "Do you know where I'd put it if it were up to me?" he asked.

They smiled politely, admitting they had no idea where he would put it if the decision were left to him.

"Come here and I'll show you," the janitor said.

Perhaps the experts needed a break and wanted to amuse themselves. In any event, they followed the janitor outside the building. "See that outside wall up there?" he asked, pointing upward. "The hallways all the way up end at that wall. Put the elevator outside the building, not inside. It won't take up extra room in the lobby, and guests will get a nice view of the city if you put windows in the elevator."

The experts dropped their patronizing smiles. The answer had been so simple and obvious that nobody had seen it. The first exterior elevator was built, and the janitor's simple solution began a nationwide trend in hotel architecture.

We all have problems at one time or another in our relationships, our health, and in our spiritual lives. They're often serious problems. But if we look at these problems honestly and thoughtfully, the solution is usually quite simple.

Phil told me his marriage with Linda was beyond repair. They spent thousands of dollars on counseling, and they attended every Christian marriage enrichment seminar that came along. The experts in marriage counseling were baffled by this couple's inability to work things out.

"I just don't respect her anymore," he told me as he ticked off a long list of her faults. But I knew that wasn't the problem because I knew something about Phil he wasn't telling the counselors or his wife.

"If you're willing to explore it, I've got an idea that will solve your problems with Linda within a week," I told him.

"I'm ready to try anything!" he replied.

"It's really quite simple: You can't think crooked and live straight. Feelings follow behavior. So stop running around on your wife with other women, and start treating her with the respect she deserves. If you treat her right, then you'll feel right about her. If you don't, eventually she's going to find out about your adolescent behavior, and you're gonna have some real problems to contend with."

As you might well imagine, he wasn't noticeably thrilled with my blunt suggestion. He wanted a complicated therapy to hide behind, perhaps something that would involve years of rooting around in the archaeology of childhood and adolescence. Something as simple as confronting his own guilt and thoughtlessness wasn't what he had in mind at all.

Most marriage problems could be solved overnight if each person spent as much time competing to *give* to his mate as he or she competes to *get*. Eventually Phil decided his wife was worth more than his immaturity, and he tried my "hairbrained" suggestion. Not surprisingly, he now enjoys a rich, rewarding relationship with his wife.

Most of our health problems have simple solutions too.

A physician friend tells the story of Ted, a middle-aged patient who came to him complaining of various problems that come with midlife. "If you want to feel good, you've got to quit smoking, get some exercise, and lose weight," the doctor said.

"Yeah, you're probably right," Ted admitted. "But I saw something in the paper about this new wonder drug. Would that help me?"

"What you need is what I said: quit smoking, exercise, and lose weight."

"What about a CAT scan?" Ted asked. "All my friends have had CAT scans."

"Maybe so. But *you* need to quit smoking, exercise, and lose weight," the doctor said patiently.

"What about my seeing a specialist at Vanderbilt? Don't they stay up on all the latest things?"

The doctor's patience was wearing thin. "I've told you what you need to do."

Ted sighed. "You're probably right, but do you mind if I get a second opinion?"

Perhaps the reason we distrust simple solutions is that we intuitively recognize there is a lot of personal responsibility behind the simplicity. This can be painfully obvious in our spiritual lives.

"Religion is just too complicated for me," Wendy complained. "You've gotta be a law school graduate to make sense out of the confusing doctrines."

She might have been surprised to know her complaint isn't new. The Old Testament prophet Micah saw the same problem. His religious leaders had an incredibly complicated system of temple worship. The rules and regulations had become more important than the people they were supposed to serve. "What is all this?" Micah asked. " 'He has showed you, O man, what is good. And what does the Lord require of you? to act justly and to love mercy and to walk humbly with your God' " (Micah 6:8).

Is that too simple? If you want to be a truly religious person, then here is a good way to begin: Do justly, love mercy, and walk humbly with God.

We don't like simple answers. We prefer answers that are worthy of our worry. We think our problems deserve complicated answers—even if they don't really answer anything. But the story of David and Goliath suggests that most of our problems—even the biggest ones—can be solved simply.

Ultimately, David got rid of all the high-tech junk of his day and used the simple weapons he had: a slingshot and some stones. They didn't look impressive as weapons. But Goliath discovered soon enough how deadly effective a slingshot can be in the right hands!

5. The J-D-I strategy

Few giants ever get talked to death. Even the best committees have to stop talking and get to work eventually. But all King Saul's soldiers ever did about Goliath was talk. They *talked* about killing him. They probably thought and prayed about it; they outlined and charted it, projected and budgeted it. They did everything but *act*.

Meanwhile, Goliath stood outside shouting insults, manifestly unimpressed with their endless debate.

I know a young woman who talks constantly about what she's going to do in the future. Every night she spends a long time writing out an elaborate, detailed list of what she's "going to do tomorrow." It's an impressive list. But there's one thing missing: She never takes any *action*.

Her giant is named Procrastination, running with a partner named Indecisiveness. The years are passing, and all she has to show for her life is a huge pile of lists she's accumulated about what she's "going to do tomorrow." Not surprisingly, she's a morose, unhappy, frustrated woman.

Do you know anybody like that? It's you and me in our unwillingness to come to terms with hard problems. It's so much easier to talk, make lists, or think about a plan than to *act* on a plan.

David's final principle in giant fighting was to get busy and do something. He wasn't impulsive. He explored the problem and listened to advice. He made sure the first four principles were clear. But then the time for talking and planning ended. He offered his services to King Saul and headed straight for Goliath without delay.

He followed the J-D-I Strategy: *Just do it!* Quit talking, analyzing, daydreaming, worrying, guessing, and arguing— *Just do it!*

For years I wanted to be a writer. I thought about it, daydreamed about the possibilities for success, planned for it, looked for opportunities—and then wrung my hands worrying about rejection because I'm a prisoner. I did everything but write. Nothing good happened until I decided, *Just do it.*

Do you want to quit smoking? Do you want to lose weight and get your body back in shape? Then, *Just do it!* If you want your joy in the Christian faith to flourish with a new vitality, ask God for help and then boldly confront the giants in your life: *Just do it!*

How do you defeat a giant? Whether that giant is named Goliath, Indifference, Greed, Ambition, Addiction, Bitterness, Anger, or whatever, David's five principles are good:

First, remember you're not alone. It's God's fight too.

Second, attack the giant at hand, not those off in the distance.

Third, use the tools you have available.

Fourth, keep it simple and don't overcomplicate things.

Fifth, begin. Do something. *Just do it!*

During my years of incarceration I've learned many helpful strategies for coping with adversity. But success is possible only when the deepest faith and the best spiritual strategies are connected with *discipline.* Without discipline such as Daniel practiced, faith disintegrates. And even the best strategy deteriorates into the kind of breathy enthusiasm that is blown away with the first stiff wind.

Ten

Building Character From the Lions' Den

Daniel's story is one of the most gripping and dramatic biographies recorded in the Old Testament. As a boy in church I vividly recall listening to my Bible teacher telling the exciting story of Daniel in the lions' den. Today, nearly forty years later, I still remember the lyric she taught us about him:

> Dare to be a Daniel;
> Dare to stand alone.
> Dare to have a purpose firm;
> Dare to make it known.

That song had a profound impact upon me as a child, but I didn't fully grasp that fact until years later in 1977, when I found myself "exiled" in prison with a ninety-nine-year prison sentence. Those song lyrics came back to me again and again as my own difficult circumstances drove me to a deeper study of what faith and courage really mean—especially when I was confronted with the roaring lions of trial and tribulation in modern life.

Although trapped in dreadful circumstances, Daniel remained a man of towering religious faith and courage throughout his life. God was so impressed with his uncompromising loyalty that toward the end of his life He sent the angel Gabriel to him with a personal message: " 'You are highly esteemed' " (Daniel 9:23).

I believe what made Daniel such an extraordinary character was the discipline he practiced. A brief review of his story puts the issue of personal discipline in perspective and shows how he translated nobility of soul into concrete terms.

Born into the royal family of King Jehoiakim, Daniel's life of luxury and privilege ended abruptly when Babylonian king Nebuchadnezzar sacked Jerusalem, looted the temple, and seized political hostages—including Daniel. Jerusalem in flames was the last thing Daniel saw as he marched off into lifelong exile.

Ordinarily, a tragic event like this would have marked the end of even the most promising young man's life. But these weren't ordinary times; God had a special message of hope He wanted delivered (see Daniel 7-12). And in one particular area—*discipline*—Daniel wasn't an ordinary man either. Because of that discipline, God's man and God's plan met at this most unpromising juncture in human history.

Trial by ordeal was a consistent theme in Daniel's life. Jealous rivals plotted his death repeatedly, and petulant kings threatened to kill him. Strong men have collapsed under far less. Why didn't he crack under the relentless pressure?

The answer is both simple and profound: Daniel possessed a truly remarkable character. But he wasn't born with it. And he didn't get this quality as a free gift from God either. Even God can't give a person character. Daniel *created* his character in the midst of the most painful circumstances by following three simple but strict disciplines throughout his life.

If you follow these three disciplines you will be able to face the lions of modern life with great success and create the kind of character in your own life that God will hold in "high esteem."

1. Disciplined in saying no

As I write this chapter, I'm sitting in the prison school where I work as an inmate teacher. During a break several prisoners were ridiculing the "Just Say No!" slogan promoted by former First Lady Nancy Reagan. Larry, another prisoner, is sitting quietly at his desk, listening to the banter.

He doesn't smile. He's dying of AIDS.

"I wish I'd just said No," he says softly, struggling with the congestion in his chest as he tries to talk and breathe at the same time. "Because I kept sticking that needle in my arm, I'm gonna die. And you're gonna die, too, if you don't smarten up."

The laughter ends abruptly. At least two of the joking convicts have shared a needle with this man. Larry died a few days later, before I finished writing this chapter.

Michelangelo was once asked how he created such magnificent statues from a chunk of cold marble. If it was an angel he was sculpting, he said, "I simply chip away everything that isn't an angel."

The word *No* is an effective chisel for chipping away everything that doesn't belong in our lives. That was Daniel's strategy for survival in Babylon. He said *No* even in something as simple as the food he ate. He knew he'd never be able to control something as complicated as his behavior if he didn't control something as elementary as what he ate.

Shortly after their arrival in Babylon, Daniel and three friends were among a select few chosen for special training and service in the king's court. This appointment was not only a great honor; as a practical matter their lives in captivity would be much easier.

But Daniel took one look at the rich, unhealthy food, and said *No!* His refusal was polite. He even suggested an alternative diet. But his answer was clear and unequivocal: *No.*

Undoubtedly, some think this a small, even a petty issue. Why create a scene—much less risk your life—over something as unimportant as food?

Let me put the question in more contemporary terms: Why risk offending friends by saying *No* to jokes that belittle women, minorities, or morality? Why tempt rejection from one's peers by saying *No* to drugs, alcohol, or cheating? Why go through the emotional firestorm of alienation from children by saying *No* to their adolescent desires?

We live in a modern age in which values are so relative that nothing is related! But Daniel was a man of clearheaded principle. He knew that moral choices are *never* petty issues. We do what we are, and we are what we believe. What we do—or refuse to do—matters, because we're creatures of deeply ingrained habit patterns that gradually evolve as the result of making many little decisions.

Long before millions of Americans were infected with a variety of sexually transmitted disease (STDs), they were infected with a bad *idea*: that the biblical commands about moral behavior are irrelevant and the lethal consequences for disobedience are not true. But some of these STDs are incurable. And AIDS is deadly!

How many of the victims suffering from STDs today wish they'd said *No* when first confronted with moral choices about sexual behavior or I.V. drug use?

How many parents wish they'd said *No* a lot more often as they watch their children coming of age, undisciplined and reckless about the way they live?

How many marriages and other relationships have been injured beyond repair because somebody didn't say *No* before angry, thoughtless words leaped from the tongue?

On the national scene we've seen the careers of prominent leaders in government and the church demolished overnight because they refused to say *No* when confronted with moral issues. And hidden behind the headlines are the wrecked lives of millions of ordinary people who believed that saying *Yes* at the wrong time was a shortcut without a cross.

But how is a Christian supposed to know what to say *No* to in this world of complex and conflicting ideas?

For Daniel, the biblical principle was clear: He said *No* to anything that was destructive to his body, mind, or soul. He knew the Bible doesn't prohibit idolatry, profanity, Sabbath breaking, murder, theft, adultery, and dishonesty because these behaviors are "bad" in some vague, abstract way; they're "bad" *because they are hurtful to people.*

I saw a magazine advertisement recently for an electronic

monitor you can install on your refrigerator. Every time you open the door a voice shouts: "Are you eating again? Close that door! You'll be sorry, *Fatty!*"

Daniel didn't need substitutes for willpower. He made some clearly defined, biblically based choices about what he wanted his life to be like and how he would live. Because of those decisions, his life became immeasurably fuller and richer as the years passed.

Every gardener knows that if you want shrubs and bushes to grow, you have to begin by cutting something off. When you prune back the dead wood, new things begin growing in its place. Building character is like that: Prune back the dead wood of self-destructive habits, and a new life you never dreamed possible will begin to sprout, flourishing with a new and unexpected vitality.

This can't be done, however, unless you have a clear picture in your mind of what you want your life to be like. Once that picture is clearly defined and framed by biblical principles, then you can identify and chip away everything that doesn't fit the picture. A firm *No*, well used, does the pruning, and remarkable things begin to grow in your character as a result.

Daniel's discipline began with his willingness to say *No*.

2. Disciplined in saying Yes

A disciplined Christian character isn't created just by saying *No*. That alone produces an obnoxious character, not a strong one.

Michelangelo's approach to sculpture was to chip away everything that didn't belong. But another method is to build up the form. Using clay or some other soft material, the artist adds layer on top of layer until the form is complete. Saying *Yes* to the right things builds up character in the same way.

But back to spiritual principles: How do we know with any reasonable degree of certainty what we should say *Yes* to? Let me suggest the implicit biblical formula Daniel followed: He said *Yes* to anything that was uplifting, healing, and nurturing for his body, mind, and soul. If some attitude or behavior nurtured the growth of his relationships with God and other people, he said *Yes*.

I think that's partly what Paul had in mind when he wrote,

"Whatever is true, whatever is noble, whatever is right, whatever is pure,whatever is lovely, whatever is admirable— if anything is excellent or praiseworthy—think about such things"—put it into practice (Philippians 4:8, 9).

These are the things to which we say *Yes!*

"I have learned this," wrote Henry David Thoreau, "that if one advances confidently in the direction of his dreams, and endeavors to lead the life which he has imagined, he will meet with a success unexpected in common hours."

By beholding Christ and imagining our lives patterned after His, we are changed. Daniel kept his eyes focused on his Lord, and he became more and more like the God he worshiped. That's how sanctification works. By saying *Yes* to the right things, that is what we will become.

But there are times when saying *Yes* is as hard as saying *No.* Saying *Yes* is what put Daniel's life at risk in the lions' den.

His habit of praying openly to God each day was well known. In order to get rid of him, jealous political rivals manipulated a vain king into passing a law that condemned to death people who prayed to any god other than the king during a thirty-day period.

Undoubtedly, friends tried to talk Daniel into sidestepping this conflict by suspending prayer altogether. "You've gotta go along to get along," they probably advised him. "At least close your window and pray privately for the next month!"

I thought about this event in Daniel's life when I faced a tough decision in 1984. Ron Freeman, a popular inmate, broke out of prison in a hail of gunfire. Other prisoners were elated by what they saw as his "spectacular triumph." In the weeks that followed, however, he left a trail of death and terror wherever he went until North Carolina lawmen finally gunned him down in a shootout.

Since I was editor of the prison newspaper, several convict leaders approached me and demanded I write an editorial that would portray Freeman as a heroic victim and the police as trigger-happy killers. They thought it would be funny to intimidate a Christian prisoner into a moral compromise out of fear of them.

"Yes, I'll write an editorial," I said finally. "But you aren't going to like it!"

111

It was the most blistering commentary I've ever published. I described Ron for what he was: a self-destructive, murdering thug who hurt and exploited everybody he touched. I warned that prisoners throughout the state would pay a high price from public backlash because of his behavior—and we did.

"Thanks a lot, Ron. We really needed this!" I concluded.

I was visited in my office the night the paper came out by three intoxicated, heavily armed, furious convicts who flung a torn-out copy of the editorial on my desk.

"What's this supposed to mean?" one man shouted as he edged around the corner of my desk.

Smoldering violence crackled in the air like static electricity. For nearly ten minutes they shouted and threatened me. But they didn't come any closer. Then they left as abruptly as they'd come. Other inmates warned that several men planned to stab me to death in the dining room when I least expected it.

Like Daniel, I could have avoided conflict by refusing to publish anything. What "practical" difference did it make whether Daniel prayed in public or solitude, whether I slanted an editorial one way or the other in a prison environment? Who would have known—or cared—one way or the other?

Daniel knew that a person who won't stand up for what he believes can't be taken seriously by God or anybody else. He flatly refused to dodge the conflict. To do that meant he'd be denying his Lord, and he wasn't about to do or say anything in the pagan kingdom that suggested God couldn't be trusted. So he put his life on the line and in God's hands by saying *Yes* to his religious convictions.

For me to remain silent was to lend tacit approval to what Freeman did. Like Daniel, I had to say a clearly defined *Yes* to values that affirmed the value of law and human life, no matter what the consequences.

Two days later one of the men came back and apologized. "I knew you were right, and so did everyone else," he said.

Happily, God protected Daniel in his lions' den and me in mine. But this experience illustrates another side to the cost of character-building discipline: saying *Yes* to the right things at the right time—regardless of the personal cost.

Daniel knew that we get where we're going by small steps.

Journeys are made and lives are created when a courageous *No* and a committed *Yes* are put together in the right combination.

3. Disciplined in being persistent

Frederick Nietzsche used a phrase that defines the issue of *persistence* clearly: "The essential thing in life is that there should be a long obedience in the same direction."

A saint does little more than the rest of us; saints are just more *persistent* at it. That's the third critically important dimension to Daniel's character-building discipline: he was *persistent* with it.

We have many one-game winning streaks. Most of us can be disciplined in short, sudden bursts of commitment. Millions of people resolve every day to quit smoking or drinking, to start an exercise or weight-reduction program, to begin daily Bible study or rejoin the church. The problem comes in sticking with it, especially when the lions of life close in around us. That's when the discipline of persistence crumbles for many.

I received a warm letter this week from a *Signs* reader who has read several of my articles and books. "I wish I knew how you retain such a strong faith in God after all these years in prison. What's your secret?"

The letter came during a particularly difficult week. While thinking about the question, I glanced at a sign posted in my office, which I think describes the experience of many people: "When you're up to your throat in snapping alligators, it's hard to remember that your original objective was to drain the swamp." I hung that sign to remind myself that even when things get tough in prison I must not forget my ultimate objective: to live a life of "long obedience" that honors God.

Prison is a world of snapping alligators! It's the most profoundly evil environment that I've ever encountered. I've spent more than 4,500 days behind the walls, and I have yet to live through *one single day* when I haven't had to contend with some aspect of human brutality, abrasiveness, hostility, and hatred. Rudeness has been cultivated to a fine art form behind these walls. Inmates routinely abuse the staff, and the staff gives as good as they get.

Both my wife and daughter have been mistreated by staff

113

members when they came to visit me. They've been subjected to sexual harassment, verbal abuse, arbitrary strip-searches, and general contempt. This inappropriate behavior is strictly against "official policy." Guards are much more careful with male visitors. But they can do just about anything they want to the women in a prisoner's family. If my wife protested or refused to submit, she would be denied access to visit me. We're not that far removed from the days of barbarism when families were killed with the prisoner!

Under these circumstances, how do you "rejoice in all things" as St. Paul commanded? How do you "turn the other cheek" as Jesus commanded? How do you hang on to beliefs about treating other people as you would be treated? How do you maintain a warm, gracious, forgiving attitude in a world where such behavior is viewed with bemused contempt? How do you continue practicing Christian virtues in such a cruel, demented environment?

These aren't abstract questions for me. I've had to struggle with them a thousand times when tempted to explode over some bizarre personal provocation. I can take any kind of abuse myself—and do quite often. But there's little that's more humiliating or degrading than being forced to stand by helplessly while my family is mistreated.

On Christmas day, when a foul-tempered officer refused to let my wife in to see me and then threatened her with arrest for demanding to see the warden, I came as close as I ever want to come to losing my mind from frustration and anger!

How do I survive? I believe what Paul said is profoundly true: "I can do everything through him who gives me strength" (Philippians 4:13). So I *persist* in what I believe to be true, regardless of how things appear from one day to the next, regardless of whether my beliefs are reviled or honored, regardless even whether God favors me in some way.

"How can I get to Mount Olympus?" Socrates was asked.

"Just make sure each step you take goes in that direction."

That's *persistence*.

There is no special "secret" to my spiritual and emotional survival; it's surprisingly, even irritatingly simple. How do you keep the heart of your faith pumping vigorously during tough times? Be *persistent*. Make sure each step you take goes in that direction. That's how we become a better husband and father. That's how we cleanse our lives of addictions and other forms of self-destructive behavior.

One reason God held Daniel in such high esteem was his disciplined *persistence*. This quality is vividly described in the first six chapters of Daniel as he confronts the challenge of adversity squarely. He refuses to eat the unhealthy food from the king's table (chapter 1). Friends follow his example and risk death in a fiery furnace because they wouldn't worship an idol (chapter 3). He doesn't gloss over God's word when it comes to warning the king of God's judgment and power (chapters 2, 4, 5). And he continues praying to God in public, even though he knows the king will have him executed for doing so (chapter 6).

Daniel persisted in *"a long obedience in the same direction"!*

Doesn't that describe the character-building process for a Christian? Isn't this how a gifted musician becomes a concert master? Isn't this how a great athlete becomes a star? Isn't this how a fulfilling marriage, a successful career, or a deep faith in God evolve?

Someone wrote a book with a provocative title, *If You Get Where You're Going, Where Will You Be?* We're all going somewhere. Every day we're *creating* our destiny by the decisions we make, and we're giving everything we have to get there—including our lives, ultimately.

But if we get where we're going, where will it be?

"If you don't know where you're going, any gust of wind will take you there," is an old piece of wisdom. But Daniel knew what he believed, and he knew the kind of life he wanted to live: one that honored God. And he knew how he wanted to be—at peace with his own integrity and with other people, and ultimately at peace with God in heaven.

After learning when to say *Yes* and when to say *No*, Daniel achieved his goal with *persistence*: "a long obedience in the same direction."

Meanwhile, back in the lions' den

Meanwhile, back in the lions' den of our own lives, we may feel that things haven't worked out quite the way we expected. Like Daniel, we said *Yes* and *No* very carefully, and we *per-*

sisted with "a long obedience in the same direction." But we still ended up in some lions' den of our own design. Life appears meaningless and purposeless. It looks as though no rescue is coming, and the lions will make a fine meal out of us.

Is it worth it, then? Does persistence in saying *Yes* and *No* really matter—then?

Years ago an old violin maker always chose the wood for his instruments from the north side of the trees because this was the side the fierce windstorms beat on. At night, when the storms came and the winds blew, the violin maker could hear the trees groaning and moaning under the lashing of the storm. But he didn't feel sorry for them. "They're simply learning to be violins," he said.

My own experience, wandering in the wilderness of a prison for the past thirteen years, has taught me this about Daniel's character-building discipline: If saying a courageous *No* and a committed *Yes* has delivered you to some persisting lions' den, God may be using the circumstances of your life to create music that no one else can make.

I've shared with you a variety of personal experiences as I've gone through my years of wandering in the wilderness of prison. I've also suggested that suffering doesn't have to leave us immobilized; by God's grace we can take steps to regain control of our lives and feelings in any set of circumstances.

I believe in taking control of a situation whenever possible. I'm not very good at standing by, doing nothing. But there comes a time when we have to learn one of the ultimate lessons in the journey of human faith: "Wait for the Lord." That's a blessing I learned during a deeply disappointing moment of my life just before Easter.

Eleven

The Message of Easter: Wait Three Days

The single most important event in all of human history took place on Easter morning when Jesus rose from the dead and left an empty tomb behind. When viewed in the light of what happened on that redemptive weekend, human existence in the midst of suffering and loss takes on a profoundly new and life-transforming meaning:

- Satan's stranglehold on humanity is broken forever.
- Impenetrable barriers to death's prison house are torn down.
- A safe and secure path to reconciliation with God's loving, redemptive grace is suddenly revealed in all of its glorious wonder.
- The power of the Holy Spirit is turned loose in the world to comfort people and draw them to God through Christ.

This truth is the focal point of any orthodox Christian faith.

But have you ever wondered *why* the disciples had to wait three days to discover that their hopes and dreams had only begun—not ended—on Golgotha? Once Jesus was pronounced dead, why didn't He step down from the cross as the risen Christ before the jeering crowd dispersed? Why did God allow Jesus' mother, disciples, and friends to suffer such terrible emotional and spiritual anguish during that historic weekend?

While I must admit that I'm always intrigued with religious Why questions, my interest is motivated by more than idle curiosity. Finding the answer to such questions is critically important for two reasons. First, every revealed act and plan of God has an important purpose, and God delights in our curiosity about His purpose. Solomon said, "It is the glory of God to conceal a matter, to search out a matter is the glory of kings" (Proverbs 25:2).

Second, every revealed plan of God has the specific purpose of ultimately blessing people in their growth, happiness, welfare, and fulfillment. " 'For I know the plans I have for you,' declares the Lord, 'plans to prosper you and not to harm you, plans to give you hope and a future' " (Jeremiah 29:11).

Although I have often puzzled over the question of *why* God made people wait three days for the resurrection, it wasn't until I experienced a traumatic disappointment of my own in 1989 that I began to grasp the significance of the three-day delay.

Learning to wait

I felt euphoric—resurrected—as Easter approached. After serving twelve *grueling* years behind prison walls, it looked as though newly uncovered evidence would lead quickly to my exoneration and freedom.

Briefly, the evidence showed that Chattanooga authorities had conspired with William H. Torbett, a known felon and indicted habitual criminal—which meant a mandatory life sentence—to commit perjury in order to obtain a conviction and ninety-nine-year prison sentence at my 1977 murder trial.

I had never met this man prior to my arrest, so I was visibly stunned when he took the stand and testified that we'd been friends for more than eighteen months, that I'd talked to him about committing a murder before it occurred, and then bragged to him later about having done it.

Although Torbett's trial had been continued past mine three times, prosecutors hotly denied any suggestion that a "secret deal" had been made with him in exchange for his testimony. In closing arguments an assistant district attorney argued that Torbett had risked his life to testify against me because he'd have to spend the rest of his life in prison as a known "snitch." That made him a credible witness, the state argued.

In fact, a deal between the state and Torbett had been cut months before my indictment. But we couldn't prove it, and the jury didn't believe it.

Six weeks after my conviction, however, the habitual criminal indictment was quietly dropped against Torbett. He was sentenced to eight years to be served in the county workhouse for two minor felonies. In June of 1978 he escaped, and I was trapped for the rest of my life—or so it appeared.

Ten years later, in October 1988, Fred Steltemeier, a Christian lawyer who six months earlier had volunteered to help me free of charge, tracked Torbett down with the aid of a Tennessee parole officer, Ed Ley.

When confronted, Torbett admitted that his testimony at my trial was totally false, given in exchange for the state's promise to drop the habitual criminal indictment. He even went so far as to name senior officials who coerced him into committing perjury. The most shocking revelation came when the escaped fugitive admitted he had been in and out of other state prisons in Texas and Alabama twice since he escaped from Tennessee. But his status as an escaped prisoner was never revealed because Chattanooga authorities had suppressed the warrant charging him with escape.

In spite of his admissions, however, Torbett refused to testify publicly without federal protection. He said he feared for his life if Chattanooga authorities were to get him in custody again.

When the U.S. attorney in Atlanta refused to investigate, Fred went directly to the Tennessee attorney general's office and laid out the facts of the case. Deputy Attorney General Jerry Smith then wrote a letter to the U.S. attorney in Knoxville, requesting a federal investigation of the facts to determine whether or not state officials had engaged in a criminal conspiracy to violate my civil rights.

A few weeks later Fred was interviewed in Chattanooga by an assistant U.S. attorney and F.B.I Special Agent Bill Curtis. They promised a thorough investigation.

"We'll have you out of there in a matter of weeks," Fred said.

I was ready to pack for departure!

Why wait three days?

But the proverbial second shoe dropped just before Easter. Agent Curtis called Fred on the telephone to say it was the opinion of the U.S. attorney that the statute of limitations had expired on any crimes that may have been committed by officials in my case. "There's nothing we can do," Curtis said. "Bragan will have to go back to court again if he ever wants to get out of prison."

I felt numb. Despair closed in around me! Like the disciples who had participated in the triumphal march into Jerusalem with Jesus, only to see Him arrested, beaten, and executed like a common criminal a week later, my burning hope for release from prison was demolished. I knew it would probably take *years* to pursue further appeals in the courts. I felt defeated.

Other times of great pain and restlessness have taught me to pace myself during periods of disappointment. Instead of surrendering to my gloomy pessimism that evening, I turned to meditating on those three days between Jesus' execution and resurrection. My reflections, however, were continually interrupted with a deeply personal question: What was the value of my lingering behind prison walls for many more years? What possible good would this accomplish for me or the world?

I didn't know the answer to that any more than I could figure out *why* Jesus lingered in the tomb for three days.

But a burning thought kept pressing upon my mind: *wait three days!* I knew God was trying to get me to think about something that connected my own sense of loss with the three days Jesus lay in the tomb. I couldn't sort through the chaos of my own feelings, so I settled down to "wait three days" and see what happened.

What happened at the end of three days? Nothing—or so I

thought at the time. It was only after reviewing this period several months later that I began to understand that three important things actually occurred as I waited during those three days.

Before exploring the implications of *why* God wanted the disciples to wait three days for the resurrection, however, follow along with me and consider *what* can happen during the three days between a cross and a new beginning. These are not only clues to the theological question; they are guiding principles to how we can move from *mourning* to *morning* in our own lives.

1. Wait three days for healing to begin

Have you ever noticed how the acute pain associated with physical injury usually subsides dramatically after three days?

Years ago, while running across the street during a sudden rainstorm, I slipped and twisted my ankle. The pain was so intense I could practically feel the throbbing in my teeth! Nevertheless, I had important business appointments to attend to, so I hobbled around for the rest of the day. By evening every nerve in my body screamed for relief, so I went to a hospital emergency room for X-rays. The ankle was broken in three places.

The doctor chuckled sympathetically when I complained about the pain as he wrapped my foot and ankle in a thick plaster cast. "I'll give you some pills," he said. "But the body is a wonderful thing—you'll feel just fine in about three days."

He was right!

When injured, the body mobilizes for a full-scale war of microscopic proportions to defend itself. White blood cells, for example, race to the scene of a cut, attacking ruthlessly any bacteria attempting to invade. Simultaneously, the brain begins manufacturing a variety of painkilling chemicals, and the cardiovascular system rushes the products throughout the body as needed.

In principle, the same phenomenon—equally invisible to the naked eye—begins when we're assaulted by the emotional and spiritual pain that follows disease, despair, and death. God rushes to our aid, sometimes directly through divine intervention, at other times through friends who gather around to comfort us or through spiritual insight gained from prior Bible study and spiritual reflection.

I don't think it's entirely a coincidence that death in our culture is usually followed by burial at the end of three days. It takes that long for the shock of loss to begin to wear off and we're at least prepared to let our loved one go in burial. Fully coming to terms with death certainly takes much longer than three days! *But the healing can begin* during that period of time for those who trust in God.

Jesus' disciples thought all was lost when they buried Him in the tomb on that terrible Friday afternoon. Their hopes and dreams were demolished. Their faith in God was badly shaken. But all around them—unseen—a war of truly cosmic proportions and eternal significance raged.

"Be strong and take heart, and wait for the Lord," the psalmist said (Psalm 27:14).

That seemed like good advice as I struggled with my own bitter disappointment at the beginning of Easter, so I decided to follow it.

Therein lies the beginning of healing in the soul.

2. Wait three days for a fresh perspective

The parents of a young college woman were stunned when they received this message from her in a letter: "Even though police say the freeway pileup was all my fault, I know you'll be relieved to hear my car wasn't damaged too badly and my cast will be off in a month.

"I was rushing to move my stuff to Raoul's house (we've decided to live together). I realize some people are prejudiced against Australian Aborigines, but I know you'll like him once you meet. Oh, and the dean said all criminal charges against Raoul should be cleared up soon."

Can you imagine what the parents were thinking at this point?

The letter then concluded: "None of the above is true. But I did get a D in English and an F in math, and I wanted you to put that fact in perspective."

When the long, dark shadows of a deeply personal Golgotha fall across your path, don't assume life is over and surrender too quickly to despair. "Wait for the Lord, and he will deliver you" (Proverbs 20:22). Because of God's promise, there is great wisdom in disciplining yourself to wait, in refusing to let the first disappointment be the final word.

Pat Barnes tells a poignant story about an Easter encounter he had with an elderly flower lady on the street. Even though she was shabbily dressed and appeared in frail health, the radiant smile on her face captivated his attention.

"You look happy this morning," he said as he picked out one of her flowers.

"Why not?" she replied. "Everything is so good."

"You wear your troubles well," Pat admitted, startled by her enthusiasm.

"When Jesus was crucified on Good Friday, that was the worst day for the whole world," she explained. "Then three days later—Easter! So when I get troubles, I've learned to wait three days. Somehow everything gets all right again."

The elderly flower lady understood perspective in light of resurrection morning!

It was on the road to Emmaus on resurrection day that the hidden Christ broke through the gloomy despair of two followers. They, too, had thought all was lost. But the risen Lord joined them and walked along with them on this universal human road of shattered hopes and dreams. When they least expected it, He gave them His presence and a fresh biblical perspective—a vision, a new way of seeing things—and their leaden emptiness was transformed into joy-filled euphoria.

The tragedy turned to triumph of resurrection morning puts everything else in perspective: Jesus is Lord! God is sovereign—no matter what happens or how things appear! God walks with us through the painful vicissitudes of life into the glorious sunshine of resurrection morning.

"The vision awaits its time. . . . If it seems slow, wait for it," Habakkuk advised (Habakkuk 3:2, RSV). Wait for the Lord. That's the beginning of a fresh perspective.

3. Wait three days for the rebirth of hope

Suffering invariably leaves us feeling lost and alone. Overwhelmed with an emotional tidal wave of despair, we're tempted to believe that these feelings will never pass.

A friend of mine used to teach wilderness survival to army special forces recruits. "If you get lost, find a river and follow it," he says. "Rivers always lead back to populated areas. And the best way to find a river is to follow the brooks and streams."

Usually, there is no great "river" of strength to help us when despair settles in after some terrible loss. But there are many small "brooks" and "streams." That means practicing those little actions of survival that enable us to get through those three days between a cross and a new beginning.

But some people make life even more painful for themselves by following the "brooks" and "streams" uphill! That's what happens when we focus every thought upon ourselves and the misery of our predicament. With each passing moment the "river" of rescue and renewal gets further and further away, and the possibility for a resurrection morning turns bleak indeed.

Harold, seventy-seven, felt lost and defeated when his wife of fifty-three years suddenly died. Each morning began as another empty and purposeless day. "I don't have any reason to live," he muttered wearily to his pastor.

"You'll never be able to overcome your feelings of loss or depression until you begin planning your life again," his pastor explained. Then he offered some practical advice about what to do when tragedy strikes. "Never end one day without something scheduled for the next," he said. "No matter how insignificant it might be, schedule something. Plan for it and anticipate it, so that the first blinks awake the following morning do not open onto an empty, purposeless day."

The disciples did the worst possible thing for themselves after their terrible disappointment: They shut themselves up in discouraged hiding. Even when the women came with the glorious news, "He's alive!" the disciples weren't prepared to accept the good news or act upon it. It's impossible to find courage, strength, and a new direction when you lock yourself in fearful isolation.

Feelings follow behavior. If you want to *feel* a renewal of hope after a terrible Friday in your life, then *behave* as though you truly expect God to bring some good out of the tragedy you've experienced. That's where faith in God's redemptive, resurrecting power plays such an important role in our lives. You've got to *believe* that the "river" is there to follow. You've got to *believe* that resurrection is waiting for you on one of those dawns yet to come.

The disciples could have stayed hidden away forever in that lonely room. So can we. Unfortunately, no one else can operate the key that opens the door and releases us from despair. We alone have it. Our attitude of hope or hopelessness determines how soon we will be delivered or how long we will stay locked in.

I felt incredibly energized when my disappointment passed after Easter, so I sat down and wrote out a seventy-three-page writ of habeas corpus and filed the appeal in Nashville's Federal District Court. I didn't have any reason to believe it would do any good. After all, three other courts had flatly rejected previous appeals. But it was the only thing left for me to do, so I did it.

I thought of David's words as I dropped the legal brief in the mailbox: "I waited patiently for the Lord; he turned to me and heard my cry. He lifted me out of the slimy pit, out of the mud and mire; he set my feet on a rock and gave me a firm place to stand." "Blessed is the man who makes the Lord his trust" (Psalm 40:1, 2, 4).

I understood what he meant!

While you wait through those three days, remember that action is potent and leads to life. Follow the brooks, if only by faith, knowing that they lead to the river. "Weeping may remain for a night, but rejoicing comes in the morning" for those who are willing to wait three days in faith for the rebirth of hope (Psalm 30:5).

From desolation to consolation

My wife, Edie, gave me a glimpse into a profound theological truth about the human journey from desolation to consolation when she went through a terrible time of loneliness and despair after her mother committed suicide. There was nothing I could do to spare Edie the pain of such a trauma. All I could do was hold her when she wept, listen to her as she talked through her feelings, and assure her that I loved her

125

and cared deeply about what she was going through.

I didn't think that was worth much at the time.

"You don't understand," she explained. "I can cope with *anything* as long as I know you love me, care about my feelings, and stick with me while I work through them."

Staggered by that thought, I realized that what she said was true of my own experience. Invariably, it's been in the midst of the worst personal desolation that I've experienced most intimately the redemptive and revitalizing consolation of Christ's presence.

St. Paul grasped this truth and wrote about it in his letter to the Hebrews: "We do not have a high priest who is unable to sympathize with our weaknesses, but we have one who has been tempted in every way, *just as we are*—yet without sin. Let us then approach the throne of grace with confidence, so that we may receive mercy and find grace to help us in our time of need" (Hebrews 4:15, 16, emphasis supplied).

Why did God have the disciples wait three days for the resurrection?

It is a truth shrouded in dazzling mystery: God in Christ suffered with us and for us on the cross. God in Christ has gone before us through the long, dark night of the soul in suffering the ultimate loss—separation from God! Because of that we can have faith in God's power to bring us emotional and spiritual healing, a radical biblical perspective that illuminates our circumstances in a new light, and the rebirth of hope in the ruins of our own tragic loss.

On September 26, 1989, I received a certified letter from the federal court where my appeal had been filed. It was a slender envelope. "It doesn't take much paper to say No," I thought as I opened it with shaking fingers.

I scanned the document until I came to these words: "ORDER: The Court finds that the petitioner (Jeris Bragan) has presented a prima facie claim of a conviction in violation of his constitutional rights."

On that lovely afternoon in the fall, dressed in a drab prison uniform and surrounded by walls, gun towers, and barbed wire, I felt the reality of God's promise for those who wait. I leaned against the stone wall and began laughing. I laughed with pure joy until the tears ran down my face, even though I knew other prisoners walking by must have wondered if I'd finally gone over the edge.

I looked up and whispered a quiet prayer of thanks. It was then that I saw a lone eagle soaring high over the prison, and I remembered a passage from the Old Testament: "They that wait on the Lord shall renew their strength; they shall mount up with wings as eagles; they shall run, and not be weary; and they shall walk, and not faint" (Isaiah 40:31, KJV).

I knew other difficult days probably lay ahead, but for me the storm was over!

IF IT WERE A NIGHTMARE, YOU COULD WAKE UP!

But for Chanla and his family, the nightmare was real.

On April 17, 1975, a savage killing machine known as the Khmer Rouge drove this well-respected family, along with thousands of others, from their home in Phnom Penh to the rice fields, where they were forced to endure backbreaking labor amid unspeakable horrors.

Salvation in the Killing Fields, by Aileen Ludington, is the gut-wrenching story of one family's desperate and deadly flight to freedom, and their life-changing encounter with Jesus Christ.

You will search long and hard for a story that can shock, move, and inspire you the way this one will. Don't miss out on the experience! Get *Salvation in the Killing Fields* today!

US$9.95/Cdn$12.45. Paper, 192 pages.
Please photocopy and complete form below.

- - - - - - - - - - - - - - - - - - - -

❏ *Salvation in the Killing Fields:* US$9.95/Cdn$12.45.
Please add applicable sales tax and 15% (US$2.50 minimum) to cover postage and handling.

Name _____

Address _____

City _____

State _____ Zip _____

Price $ _____   Order from your local Christian bookstore or ABC Mailing Service, P.O. Box 7000, Boise, Idaho 83707. Prices subject to change without notice. Make check payable to Pacific Press.

Postage $ _____

Sales Tax $ _____

TOTAL $ _____

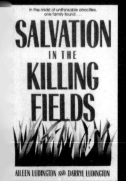

In the midst of unthinkable atrocities, one family found . . .

SALVATION IN THE KILLING FIELDS

AILEEN LUDINGTON AND DARRYL LUDINGTON

© 1990 Pacific Press Publishing Association 2227